YOUR PERSONAL ENGLISH ORGANISER

STEVE SMITH AND JACQUELINE SMITH

with additional material by
GAIL ELLIS AND BARBARA SINCLAIR
RICHARD ACKLAM

Learning techniques by Gail Ellis and Barbara Sinclair
Grammar strategies by Gail Ellis and Barbara Sinclair
Grammar by Richard Acklam

The publishers and authors would like to thank all those who have contributed advice to the development of *Wordflo*, in particular the Editorial Advisory Board: Rod Bolitho (College of St Mark and St John, Plymouth), Duncan Campbell (Central School of English, London), Olivia Date, Gail Ellis, Lisa Hale (St Giles College, London) and Susan Sheerin (Bell Language School, Cambridge). Our thanks are also due to Susan Maingay (The British Council, Poland), Gabriel Mulcauley, Stella O'Shea and Jayne West.

We would also like to thank the many teachers and students who helped in the development and piloting of *Wordflo*: The Director and teaching staff of the British Schools of Pisa and Livorno, Italy, the Director and teaching staff of the Center for English Studies, New York, Richard Denys (Bell Language School, Cambridge), Patricia Lynch, Lesley Mackie, Andrea Robert-Dantec (CIEL, Le Relecq Kerhuon, France) Janice Feche and Guberina Luerka (Créalangues, Paris), Brett Hawthorne (Devon School of English), Felicity Chatham, Jenny Djeddour (English Language Teaching Centre, UMIST, Manchester), Peter Clarke, Peter Umney-Gray (Suzanne Sparrow (Plymouth) Language School).
The authors would also like to thank *The Reporter*, Florence, Italy.

PERSONAL INFORMATION

Name
Address
Tel

School/Company

Name
Address
Tel
Fax
English teacher's name
Class

Important dates

Start of English course
End of English course
Tests/Exams
Holidays
Other

Organise your learning

© Addison Wesley Longman Limited 1998

wordflo

Photocopiable

MONDAY	TUESDAY	WEDNESDAY	THURSDAY	FRIDAY	SATURDAY	SUNDAY

wordflo
© Addison Wesley Longman Limited 1998

PLANNER

Plan your Wordflo time

MONDAY	
TUESDAY	
WEDNESDAY	
THURSDAY	
FRIDAY	
SATURDAY	
SUNDAY	

Wordflo
© Addison Wesley Longman Limited 1998

WORDFLO CALENDARS

January 1998
Wk	M	T	W	T	F	S	S
1	–	–	–	1	2	3	4
2	5	6	7	8	9	10	11
3	12	13	14	15	16	17	18
4	19	20	21	22	23	24	25
5	26	27	28	29	30	31	–

February 1998
Wk	M	T	W	T	F	S	S
6	–	–	–	–	–	–	1
7	2	3	4	5	6	7	8
8	9	10	11	12	13	14	15
9	16	17	18	19	20	21	22
10	23	24	25	26	27	28	–

March 1998
Wk	M	T	W	T	F	S	S
10	–	–	–	–	–	–	1
11	2	3	4	5	6	7	8
12	9	10	11	12	13	14	15
13	16	17	18	19	20	21	22
14	23	24	25	26	27	28	29
14	30	31	–	–	–	–	–

April 1998
Wk	M	T	W	T	F	S	S
14	–	–	1	2	3	4	5
15	6	7	8	9	10	11	12
16	13	14	15	16	17	18	19
17	20	21	22	23	24	25	26
18	27	28	29	30	–	–	–

May 1998
Wk	M	T	W	T	F	S	S
18	–	–	–	–	1	2	3
19	4	5	6	7	8	9	10
20	11	12	13	14	15	16	17
21	18	19	20	21	22	23	24
22	25	26	27	28	29	30	31

June 1998
Wk	M	T	W	T	F	S	S
23	1	2	3	4	5	6	7
24	8	9	10	11	12	13	14
25	15	16	17	18	19	20	21
26	22	23	24	25	26	27	28
27	29	30	–	–	–	–	–

July 1998
Wk	M	T	W	T	F	S	S
27	–	–	1	2	3	4	5
28	6	7	8	9	10	11	12
29	13	14	15	16	17	18	19
30	20	21	22	23	24	25	26
31	27	28	29	30	31	–	–

August 1998
Wk	M	T	W	T	F	S	S
31	–	–	–	–	–	1	2
32	3	4	5	6	7	8	9
33	10	11	12	13	14	15	16
34	17	18	19	20	21	22	23
35	24	25	26	27	28	29	30
36	31	–	–	–	–	–	–

September 1998
Wk	M	T	W	T	F	S	S
36	–	1	2	3	4	5	6
37	7	8	9	10	11	12	13
38	14	15	16	17	18	19	20
39	21	22	23	24	25	26	27
40	28	29	30	–	–	–	–

October 1998
Wk	M	T	W	T	F	S	S
40	–	–	–	1	2	3	4
41	5	6	7	8	9	10	11
42	12	13	14	15	16	17	18
43	19	20	21	22	23	24	25
44	26	27	28	29	30	31	–

November 1998
Wk	M	T	W	T	F	S	S
44	–	–	–	–	–	–	1
45	2	3	4	5	6	7	8
46	9	10	11	12	13	14	15
47	16	17	18	19	20	21	22
48	23	24	25	26	27	28	29
49	30	–	–	–	–	–	–

December 1998
Wk	M	T	W	T	F	S	S
49	–	1	2	3	4	5	6
50	7	8	9	10	11	12	13
51	14	15	16	17	18	19	20
52	21	22	23	24	25	26	27
53	28	29	30	31	–	–	–

January 1999
Wk	M	T	W	T	F	S	S
1	–	–	–	–	1	2	3
2	4	5	6	7	8	9	10
3	11	12	13	14	15	16	17
4	18	19	20	21	22	23	24
5	25	26	27	28	29	30	31

February 1999
Wk	M	T	W	T	F	S	S
6	1	2	3	4	5	6	7
7	8	9	10	11	12	13	14
8	15	16	17	18	19	20	21
9	22	23	24	25	26	27	28

March 1999
Wk	M	T	W	T	F	S	S
10	1	2	3	4	5	6	7
11	8	9	10	11	12	13	14
12	15	16	17	18	19	20	21
13	22	23	24	25	26	27	28
14	29	30	31	–	–	–	–

April 1999
Wk	M	T	W	T	F	S	S
14	–	–	–	1	2	3	4
15	5	6	7	8	9	10	11
16	12	13	14	15	16	17	18
17	19	20	21	22	23	24	25
18	26	27	28	29	30	–	–

May 1999
Wk	M	T	W	T	F	S	S
18	–	–	–	–	–	1	2
19	3	4	5	6	7	8	9
20	10	11	12	13	14	15	16
21	17	18	19	20	21	22	23
22	24	25	26	27	28	29	30
23	31	–	–	–	–	–	–

June 1999
Wk	M	T	W	T	F	S	S
23	–	1	2	3	4	5	6
24	7	8	9	10	11	12	13
25	14	15	16	17	18	19	20
26	21	22	23	24	25	26	27
27	28	29	30	–	–	–	–

July 1999
Wk	M	T	W	T	F	S	S
27	–	–	–	1	2	3	4
28	5	6	7	8	9	10	11
29	12	13	14	15	16	17	18
30	19	20	21	22	23	24	25
31	26	27	28	29	30	31	–

August 1999
Wk	M	T	W	T	F	S	S
31	–	–	–	–	–	–	1
32	2	3	4	5	6	7	8
33	9	10	11	12	13	14	15
34	16	17	18	19	20	21	22
35	23	24	25	26	27	28	29
36	30	31	–	–	–	–	–

September 1999
Wk	M	T	W	T	F	S	S
36	–	–	1	2	3	4	5
37	6	7	8	9	10	11	12
38	13	14	15	16	17	18	19
39	20	21	22	23	24	25	26
40	27	28	29	30	–	–	–

October 1999
Wk	M	T	W	T	F	S	S
40	–	–	–	–	1	2	3
41	4	5	6	7	8	9	10
42	11	12	13	14	15	16	17
43	18	19	20	21	22	23	24
44	25	26	27	28	29	30	31

November 1999
Wk	M	T	W	T	F	S	S
45	1	2	3	4	5	6	7
46	8	9	10	11	12	13	14
47	15	16	17	18	19	20	21
48	22	23	24	25	26	27	28
49	29	30	–	–	–	–	–

December 1999
Wk	M	T	W	T	F	S	S
49	–	–	1	2	3	4	5
50	6	7	8	9	10	11	12
51	13	14	15	16	17	18	19
52	20	21	22	23	24	25	26
53	27	28	29	30	31	–	–

wordflo
© Addison Wesley Longman Limited 1998

YOUR GUIDE TO SUCCESSFUL LANGUAGE LEARNING

- Find out what you like doing and why.
- Find out what you need to do and why.
- Be realistic about how much time you have for learning English.
- Work out what you can do in the time you have.
- Make good use of the resources around you, e.g. your dictionary, a good grammar book, cassettes, videos, books, magazines and your teacher.
- Plan your learning.
- Practise often and regularly.
- Take risks – don't worry all the time about making mistakes.
- Review often and regularly.
- Find out your strong and weak points.
- Decide what you need to do next.

TIPS

© Addison Wesley Longman Limited 1998

wordflo

QUIZ

How do you like to learn?

Everyone is different. People learn languages in different ways because they have different learning styles. Think about how you like to learn. This will help you become a better learner of English.

Are you someone who:

a) likes your teacher to tell you what to do and to correct every mistake you make? Why?

b) likes learning grammar rules and enjoys analysing language? Why?

c) likes playing language games with other students in class and doesn't like doing the same thing all the time? Why?

d) likes talking to people and doesn't worry about making mistakes? Why?

e) likes to learn in more than one of these ways? Why?

f) is not sure how you like to learn? Why not?

Think and grow with Wordflo!

Advice

← Try to *depend on yourself* more.

← Don't forget to use your language, too.

← Try to spend some time *studying*, as well, or you won't feel you are making progress.

← Try to *notice your mistakes* so you can learn from them and be correct next time.

← Read the advice above and *think* about how it can help you.

← Read the quiz and the advice again. *Think* about these as you do the activities in *Wordflo*, and you will begin to find out more about how you like to learn.

WHAT CAN YOU DO TO LEARN ENGLISH?

It is important to have a general learning strategy when you learn English:

PLAN → DO → REVIEW

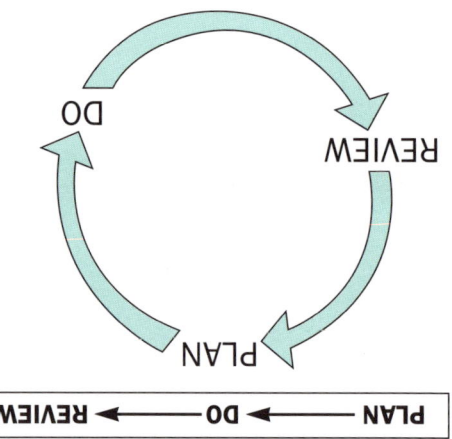

PLAN
– what you need to do
– your learning time
– your resources (dictionary, grammar book, cassettes, videos, books, magazines, your teacher etc.)
– your vocabulary or grammar strategy
– your review time

DO
– your plan
– your language learning or practice activity

REVIEW
– what you did
– why you did it
– how well you did
– what you need to do next

PLAN → DO → REVIEW again.

PLAN

WHAT DO YOU NEED TO DO?

Wordflo helps you improve your English vocabulary and grammar learning. A good knowledge of vocabulary and grammar is essential for your listening, speaking, reading and writing.

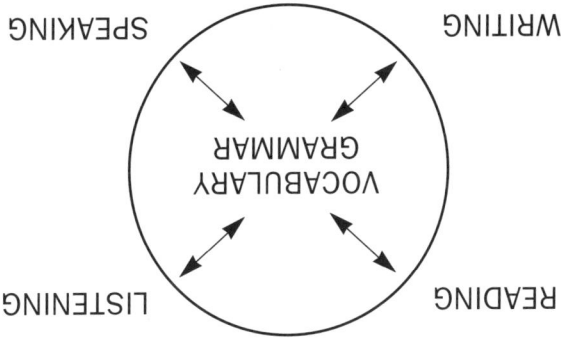

Listening, speaking, reading and writing in English will also help you to improve your vocabulary and grammar.

What do you need English for?

☐ your job
☐ travel
☐ your studies
☐ other

What vocabulary do you need?

List the specific topics and situations.
For example: at the airport, at the bank, houses...

....
....
....
....
....
....
....
....

Find out what you need to do and why

What grammar do you need?

List the grammar you need. For example: *question forms in the Present simple and Past simple.*

....
....
....
....

PLAN YOUR LEARNING TIME

Most people have busy lives and do not have much time for learning English. Find out how much time you have for learning English.

Calculate your *Wordflo* time

There are 168 hours in a week. Calculate how many hours you spend doing the following things in a typical week to find out how much time you have for *Wordflo*.

ACTIVITY	HOURS
sleeping	
washing and dressing	
shopping	
housework	
caring for others	
work / study	
leisure activities	
eating	
travelling	
TOTAL	
168 hours – TOTAL = *Wordflo* time	

Do you need more *Wordflo* time?
If yes, how can you make more *Wordflo* time?
Use your *Wordflo* Planner to schedule *Wordflo* time.

Decide what you can do in the time you have. Be realistic!

WHAT RESOURCES DO YOU NEED?

- Have you got a good bilingual dictionary?
- Have you got a good monolingual dictionary?
  ▶ See **Dictionary skills**.
- Have you got a good grammar book?
- Find out about other resources, for example, TV, videos, radio, magazines, newspapers, books, people etc.
- Do you ask your teacher questions?
- Have you decided which **Data systems** are best for you?

Use your *Wordflo*!

SELECT YOUR STRATEGY

Strategies are the techniques you use to learn something. There are many strategies for language learning. Try different strategies and select the ones you prefer and which work best for you.

You will find some vocabulary strategies on the first pages of the **Vocabulary** section, and grammar strategies on the first pages of the **Grammar** section in *Wordflo*. Select a strategy to try.

Over the next few weeks, try other strategies to find out which ones help you to learn best.

Make good use of the resources around you, including your teacher.

PLAN YOUR REVIEW TIME

Reviewing (looking back at what you have done) is important for successful learning. If you want to remember what you have learnt, it is necessary to review often and regularly.

Do you know the best time to review? Look at the graph:

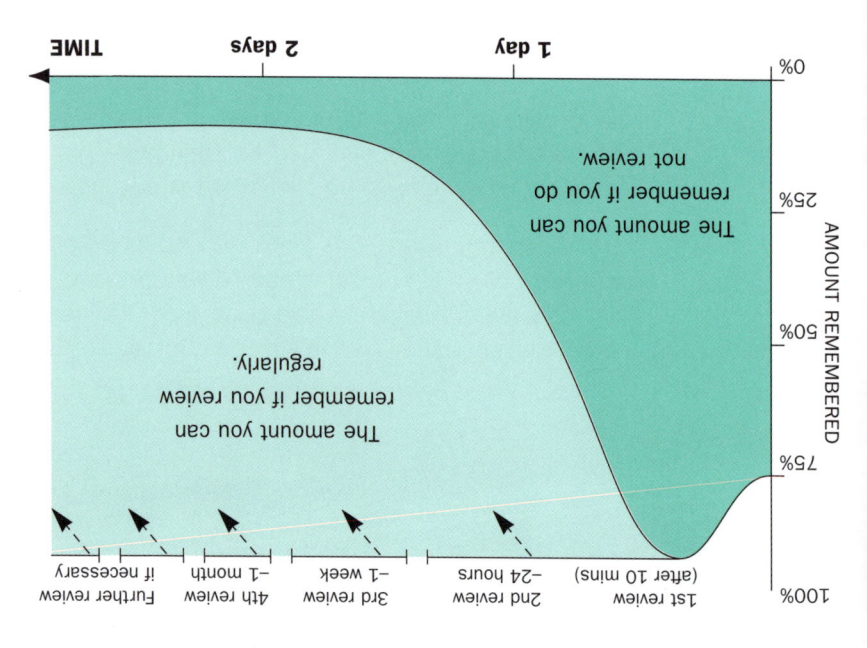

- 1st review (after 10 mins)
- 2nd review –24 hours
- 3rd review –1 week
- 4th review –1 month
- Further review if necessary

The amount you can remember if you review regularly.

The amount you can remember if you do not review.

AMOUNT REMEMBERED: 0%, 25%, 50%, 75%, 100%
TIME: 1 day, 2 days

Plan review sessions into your *Wordflo* time.

Review often and regularly!

DO

Read about Françoise and look at her learning plan.

Françoise

'I am a student in France. I am going on a study trip to Britain and I need to learn more vocabulary for my trip.'

This is Françoise's plan.

WHAT TO STUDY?	WORDFLO TIME	RESOURCES	STRATEGY	REVIEW TIME	DONE
Vocab about a study trip abroad	Monday, 3rd Feb: 9–9.30 pm	Wordflo Dictionaries	Word web	Review 1: 9.30–9.40 pm	✓
				Review 2: Tuesday 4th Feb: 9.30 pm	✓
				Review 3: Monday 10th Feb: 9.30 pm	✓

What strategies would you use to learn vocabulary for a study trip abroad?

Find out what you like doing and why

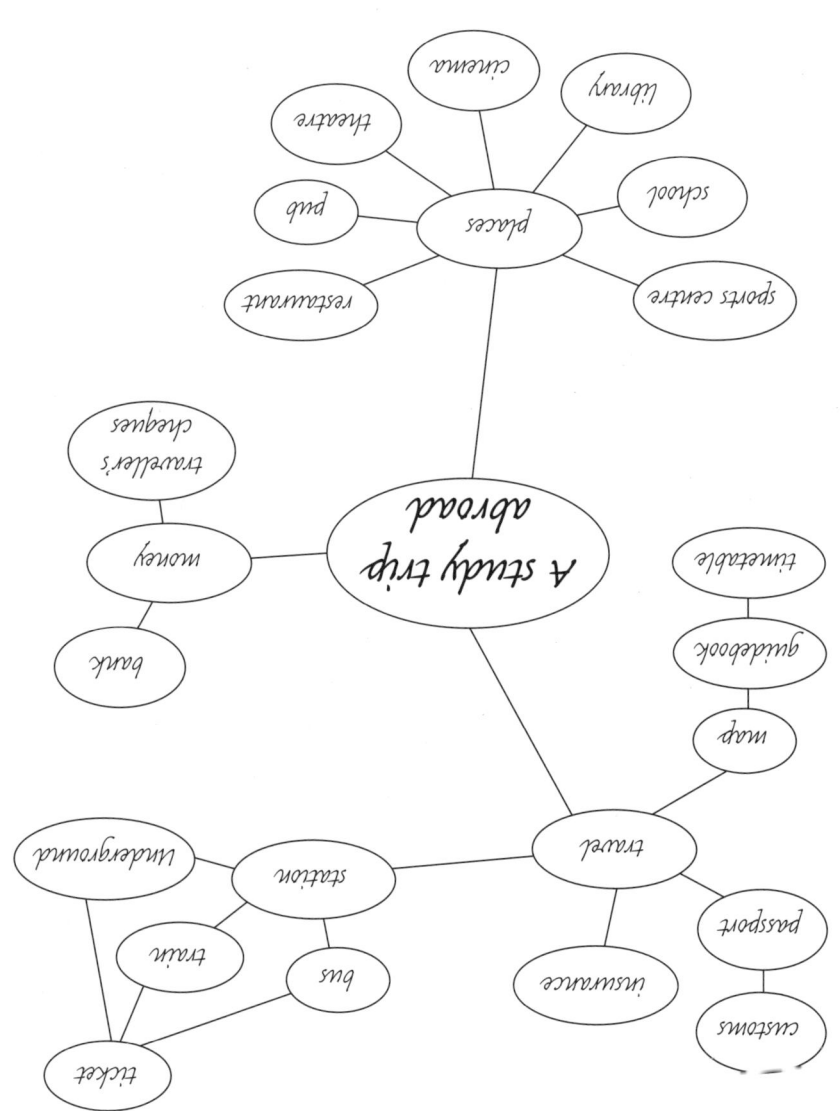

Here is Françoise's activity. She has selected a Word web.

Photocopiable

Try using a chart like this from time to time to study

WHAT?	WORDFLO TIME	RESOURCES	STRATEGY	REVIEW TIME	DONE

Use this chart to do your plan.

wordflo
© Addison Wesley Longman Limited 1998

WHAT?	WORDFLO TIME	RESOURCES	STRATEGY	REVIEW TIME	DONE

REVIEW

What did you do?

'I learned vocabulary for a study trip abroad.'

What strategy did you use?

'A Word web. I enjoyed doing it. First, I looked at the example in Wordflo to see how to do it. I looked at the study trip brochure for new words. Then I looked them up in my dictionaries and wrote them in my Word web. I enjoyed thinking about how to group the words.'

Why did you do it?

'I usually write words down with their translation, but I still have problems remembering them. I wanted to try something new. Also, I like drawing diagrams.'

How well did you do?

'At first, I found it difficult to know where to write the words. I had to think hard, but this helped me to remember the words. I can see the Word web in my mind.'

What do you need to do next?

'I like the idea of grouping words to learn them, so I'm going to use the Topics Data system to collect words about 'going to the bank' and 'going to the library'.'

Review often and regularly

© Addison Wesley Longman Limited 1998

WHAT DID YOU DO?	WHAT STRATEGY DID YOU USE?	WHY DID YOU DO IT?	HOW WELL DID YOU DO?	WHAT DO YOU NEED TO DO NEXT?
Learned words for study trip to Britain	Word web	To learn and remember words	A good strategy for me!	Add more words to my Word web
		To find a better strategy	It helped me remember the words	Try Topics Data system
		I like diagrams		Do more Word webs!!

Françoise has now completed her review chart:

Photocopiable

Decide what you need to do next!

WHAT DID YOU DO?	WHAT STRATEGY DID YOU USE?	WHY DID YOU DO IT?	HOW WELL DID YOU DO?	WHAT DO YOU NEED TO DO NEXT?

Use this chart to review your learning.
Try using a chart like this from time to time.

Wordflo
© Addison Wesley Longman Limited 1998

MAKING PROGRESS

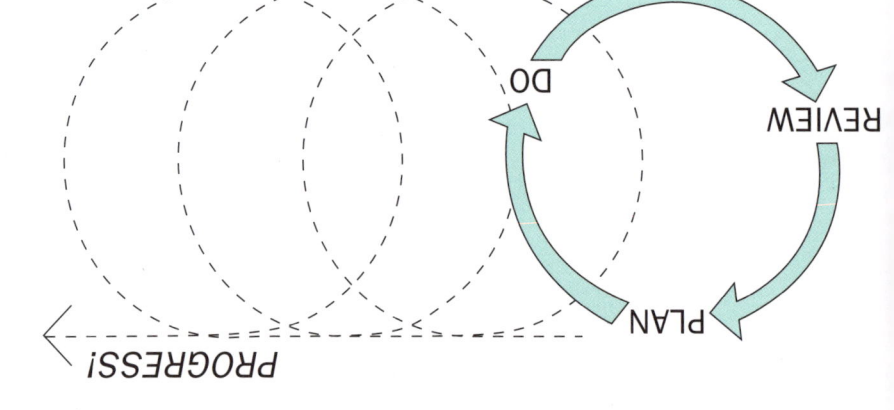

When you have completed the PLAN ➔ DO ➔ REVIEW cycle

PLAN ➔ DO ➔ REVIEW again!

PROGRESS!

PLAN ➔ REVIEW ➔ DO (cycle diagram)

If you use the PLAN ➔ DO ➔ REVIEW general learning strategy regularly, you will see your progress.

Give yourself a reward!

© Addison Wesley Longman Limited 1998

WHY *WORDFLO* WILL HELP YOU TO LEARN ENGLISH

It's easier to learn English when you have a system. *Wordflo* is that system.

Organising

It's a good idea to write notes when you are learning English to help you remember. But you need to organise your notes to find them again quickly and easily. *Wordflo* will help you organise your learning.

Personalising

Wordflo is your personal English language organiser. You can write the information that is most important for *you*.

Growing

You will be able to use *Wordflo* for many years. You can add the new vocabulary, grammar and phrases you learn. *Wordflo* will grow and change with your knowledge of English.

HOW TO USE *WORDFLO*

Look through *Wordflo*. Find out what it contains.

Read the section on **Learning techniques** carefully. It gives useful information on how to learn.

You will see that a lot of the pages are blank. Don't try to complete these **Data systems** immediately. You can write something one day and then go back and add more – two days, two months, or two years later.

Look at all the different parts of *Wordflo*. Then decide which ones are the most useful for you.

Use the **Notes** section when you need to write down something quickly, (for example, when you hear an interesting expression in class or on a video). Later you can put your notes in one of the **Data systems**.

WHEN TO USE *WORDFLO*

Take *Wordflo* to English lessons.

Take *Wordflo* with you when you need to speak English, for example, when you travel.

Keep *Wordflo* with you when you watch a film on television or a video in English.

You will soon see what a difference *Wordflo* makes to your English!

Photocopiable

Photocopiable

Remember to write your notes later in the **Data systems**

Photocopiable

© Addison Wesley Longman Limited 1998

Photocopiable

Organise your learning

Photocopiable

© Addison Wesley Longman Limited 1998

wordflo
© Addison Wesley Longman Limited 1998

Photocopiable

Learning is easy when you have a system

Wordflo
© Addison Wesley Longman Limited 1998

Photocopiable

NOTES

Use the Notes section when you need to write down something quickly, for example, when you hear a new word or expression in class. Later you can write your notes in one of the Data systems.

Write down the words which are important to you

NOTES

NOTES

NOTES

NOTES

Photocopiable

NOTES

NOTES

NOTES

NOTES

Photocopiable

Learning vocabulary is easy when you have a system

EXAMPLE SENTENCE	MEANING/TRANSLATION

EXAMPLE SENTENCE	MEANING/TRANSLATION

Photocopiable

Review often and regularly

EXAMPLE SENTENCE	MEANING/TRANSLATION

EXAMPLE SENTENCE	MEANING/TRANSLATION

Photocopiable

Photocopiable

Write about topics that are important to you

Wordflo
© Addison Wesley Longman Limited 1998

Photocopiable

Photocopiable

Add pronunciation where you think it is useful

WORD/EXPRESSION PRONUNCIATION	PART OF SPEECH	PICTURE, MEANING OR TRANSLATION	EXAMPLE SENTENCE	NOTES

Wordflo
© Addison Wesley Longman Limited 1998

Photocopiable

WORD/EXPRESSION PRONUNCIATION	PART OF SPEECH	PICTURE, MEANING OR TRANSLATION	EXAMPLE SENTENCE	NOTES

Photocopiable

Review often and regularly

WORD/EXPRESSION PRONUNCIATION	PART OF SPEECH	PICTURE, MEANING OR TRANSLATION	EXAMPLE SENTENCE	NOTES

Wordflo
© Addison Wesley Longman Limited 1998

Photocopiable

WORD/EXPRESSION PRONUNCIATION	PART OF SPEECH	PICTURE, MEANING OR TRANSLATION	EXAMPLE SENTENCE	NOTES

Photocopiable

Organise your learning!

WORD/EXPRESSION PRONUNCIATION	PART OF SPEECH	PICTURE, MEANING OR TRANSLATION	EXAMPLE SENTENCE	NOTES

Photocopiable

© Addison Wesley Longman Limited 1998

WORD/EXPRESSION PRONUNCIATION	PART OF SPEECH	PICTURE, MEANING OR TRANSLATION	EXAMPLE SENTENCE	NOTES

You can write opposites in the Notes column

WORD/EXPRESSION PRONUNCIATION	PART OF SPEECH	PICTURE, MEANING OR TRANSLATION	EXAMPLE SENTENCE	NOTES

WORD/EXPRESSION PRONUNCIATION	PART OF SPEECH	PICTURE, MEANING OR TRANSLATION	EXAMPLE SENTENCE	NOTES

Photocopiable

You can write opposites in the Notes column

WORD/EXPRESSION PRONUNCIATION	PART OF SPEECH	PICTURE, MEANING OR TRANSLATION	EXAMPLE SENTENCE	NOTES

WORD/EXPRESSION PRONUNCIATION	PART OF SPEECH	PICTURE, MEANING OR TRANSLATION	EXAMPLE SENTENCE	NOTES

Photocopiable

Use your dictionary to check spelling and pronunciation

WORD/EXPRESSION PRONUNCIATION	PART OF SPEECH	PICTURE, MEANING OR TRANSLATION	EXAMPLE SENTENCE	NOTES

Photocopiable

WORD/EXPRESSION PRONUNCIATION	PART OF SPEECH	PICTURE, MEANING OR TRANSLATION	EXAMPLE SENTENCE	NOTES

Photocopiable

Use your dictionary to check spelling and pronunciation

WORD/EXPRESSION PRONUNCIATION	PART OF SPEECH	PICTURE, MEANING OR TRANSLATION	EXAMPLE SENTENCE	NOTES

WORD/EXPRESSION PRONUNCIATION	PART OF SPEECH	PICTURE, MEANING OR TRANSLATION	EXAMPLE SENTENCE	NOTES

Write example sentences about your life and interests

WORD/EXPRESSION PRONUNCIATION	PART OF SPEECH	PICTURE, MEANING OR TRANSLATION	EXAMPLE SENTENCE	NOTES

WORD/EXPRESSION PRONUNCIATION	PART OF SPEECH	PICTURE, MEANING OR TRANSLATION	EXAMPLE SENTENCE	NOTES

Write example sentences about your life and interests

WORD/EXPRESSION PRONUNCIATION	PART OF SPEECH	PICTURE, MEANING OR TRANSLATION	EXAMPLE SENTENCE	NOTES

WORD/EXPRESSION PRONUNCIATION	PART OF SPEECH	PICTURE, MEANING OR TRANSLATION	EXAMPLE SENTENCE	NOTES

Photocopiable

Writing things down helps you to remember them

WORD/EXPRESSION PRONUNCIATION	PART OF SPEECH	PICTURE, MEANING OR TRANSLATION	EXAMPLE SENTENCE	NOTES

Photocopiable

WORD/EXPRESSION PRONUNCIATION	PART OF SPEECH	PICTURE, MEANING OR TRANSLATION	EXAMPLE SENTENCE	NOTES

Photocopiable

Writing things down helps you to remember them

WORD/EXPRESSION PRONUNCIATION	PART OF SPEECH	PICTURE, MEANING OR TRANSLATION	EXAMPLE SENTENCE	NOTES

Photocopiable

WORD/EXPRESSION PRONUNCIATION	PART OF SPEECH	PICTURE, MEANING OR TRANSLATION	EXAMPLE SENTENCE	NOTES

Photocopiable

Organise your learning!

WORD/EXPRESSION PRONUNCIATION	PART OF SPEECH	PICTURE, MEANING OR TRANSLATION	EXAMPLE SENTENCE	NOTES

Photocopiable

WORD/EXPRESSION PRONUNCIATION	PART OF SPEECH	PICTURE, MEANING OR TRANSLATION	EXAMPLE SENTENCE	NOTES

Photocopiable

Organise your learning!

WORD/EXPRESSION PRONUNCIATION	PART OF SPEECH	PICTURE, MEANING OR TRANSLATION	EXAMPLE SENTENCE	NOTES

WORD/EXPRESSION PRONUNCIATION	PART OF SPEECH	PICTURE, MEANING OR TRANSLATION	EXAMPLE SENTENCE	NOTES

Photocopiable

You can write opposites in the Notes column

WORD/EXPRESSION PRONUNCIATION	PART OF SPEECH	PICTURE, MEANING OR TRANSLATION	EXAMPLE SENTENCE	NOTES

Wordflo
© Addison Wesley Longman Limited 1998

WORD/EXPRESSION PRONUNCIATION	PART OF SPEECH	PICTURE, MEANING OR TRANSLATION	EXAMPLE SENTENCE	NOTES

Photocopiable

You can write opposites in the Notes column

WORD/EXPRESSION PRONUNCIATION	PART OF SPEECH	PICTURE, MEANING OR TRANSLATION	EXAMPLE SENTENCE	NOTES

Wordflo
© Addison Wesley Longman Limited 1998

Photocopiable

WORD/EXPRESSION PRONUNCIATION	PART OF SPEECH	PICTURE, MEANING OR TRANSLATION	EXAMPLE SENTENCE	NOTES

Photocopiable

Does your word/expression start with G or H?

WORD/EXPRESSION PRONUNCIATION	PART OF SPEECH	PICTURE, MEANING OR TRANSLATION	EXAMPLE SENTENCE	NOTES

WORD/EXPRESSION PRONUNCIATION	PART OF SPEECH	PICTURE, MEANING OR TRANSLATION	EXAMPLE SENTENCE	NOTES

Photocopiable

Does your word/expression start with G or H?

WORD/EXPRESSION PRONUNCIATION	PART OF SPEECH	PICTURE, MEANING OR TRANSLATION	EXAMPLE SENTENCE	NOTES

WORD/EXPRESSION PRONUNCIATION	PART OF SPEECH	PICTURE, MEANING OR TRANSLATION	EXAMPLE SENTENCE	NOTES

Photocopiable

Review often and regularly

WORD/EXPRESSION PRONUNCIATION	PART OF SPEECH	PICTURE, MEANING OR TRANSLATION	EXAMPLE SENTENCE	NOTES

Photocopiable

© Addison Wesley Longman Limited 1998

WORD/EXPRESSION PRONUNCIATION	PART OF SPEECH	PICTURE, MEANING OR TRANSLATION	EXAMPLE SENTENCE	NOTES

Photocopiable

Review often and regularly

WORD/EXPRESSION PRONUNCIATION	PART OF SPEECH	PICTURE, MEANING OR TRANSLATION	EXAMPLE SENTENCE	NOTES

Photocopiable

WORD/EXPRESSION PRONUNCIATION	PART OF SPEECH	PICTURE, MEANING OR TRANSLATION	EXAMPLE SENTENCE	NOTES

Photocopiable

Remember to use the Notes column

WORD/EXPRESSION PRONUNCIATION	PART OF SPEECH	PICTURE, MEANING OR TRANSLATION	EXAMPLE SENTENCE	NOTES

Photocopiable

© Addison Wesley Longman Limited 1998

WORD/EXPRESSION PRONUNCIATION	PART OF SPEECH	PICTURE, MEANING OR TRANSLATION	EXAMPLE SENTENCE	NOTES

Photocopiable

Remember to use the Notes column

WORD/EXPRESSION PRONUNCIATION	PART OF SPEECH	PICTURE, MEANING OR TRANSLATION	EXAMPLE SENTENCE	NOTES

WORD/EXPRESSION PRONUNCIATION	PART OF SPEECH	PICTURE, MEANING OR TRANSLATION	EXAMPLE SENTENCE	NOTES

Photocopiable

Use your dictionary to check spelling and pronunciation

WORD/EXPRESSION PRONUNCIATION	PART OF SPEECH	PICTURE, MEANING OR TRANSLATION	EXAMPLE SENTENCE	NOTES

Photocopiable

WORD/EXPRESSION PRONUNCIATION	PART OF SPEECH	PICTURE, MEANING OR TRANSLATION	EXAMPLE SENTENCE	NOTES

Photocopiable

Use your dictionary to check spelling and pronunciation

Photocopiable

© Addison Wesley Longman Limited 1998
Wordflo

Photocopiable

Remember to write your notes later in the **Data systems**

Photocopiable

© Addison Wesley Longman Limited 1998
Wordflo

© Addison Wesley Longman Limited 1998

Photocopiable

Learning is easy when you have a system

Photocopiable

© Addison Wesley Longman Limited 1998

© Addison Wesley Longman Limited 1998

Photocopiable

Remember to write your notes later in the **Data systems**

Photocopiable

© Addison Wesley Longman Limited 1998

© Addison Wesley Longman Limited 1998
wordflo

Photocopiable

Learning is easy when you have a system
wf

Addison Wesley Longman Limited
Edinburgh Gate, Harlow,
Essex CM20 2JE, England
and Associated Companies throughout the World.

© Addison Wesley Longman Limited 1998
All rights reserved; no part of this publication may be reproduced, stored in a retrieval system, or transmitted in any form or by any means, electronic, mechanical, photocopying, recording, or otherwise without the prior written permission of the Publishers.

First published 1998
Third impression 1998

Wordflo is trademark of Addison Wesley Longman Limited

Photocopying

The Publishers grant permission for the photocopying of those pages marked 'photocopiable' according to the following conditions. Individual purchasers may make copies for their own use or for use by classes they teach, but this permission does not extend to additional schools or branches.

Under no circumstances may any part of this book be photocopied for resale.

Set in Franklin Gothic, New Caflisch
Printed in China
SK/03

ISBN 0582 33540 X

wordflo™

YOUR PERSONAL ENGLISH ORGANISER

REFILL PACK

ISBN 0-582-33540-X

LONGMAN

Addison Wesley Longman Limited
Edinburgh Gate, Harlow,
Essex CM20 2JE, England
and Associated Companies throughout the World.

© Addison Wesley Longman Limited 1998
All rights reserved; no part of this publication may be reproduced, stored in a retrieval system, or transmitted in any form or by any means, electronic, mechanical, photocopying, recording, or otherwise, without the prior written permission of the Publisher.

First published 1998
Third impression 1998

Wordflo is a trademark of Addison Wesley Longman Limited

Photocopying

The Publishers grant permission for the photocopying of those pages marked 'photocopiable' according to the following conditions. Individual purchasers may make copies for their own use or for use by classes they teach, but this permission does not extend to additional schools or branches.

Under no circumstances may any part of this book be photocopied for resale.

Set in Franklin Gothic, New Caflisch
Printed in China
SK/03

ISBN 0582 303028

Designed by Shireen Nathoo Design

The publishers wish to thank Rosi Jillett for her editorial input on this title.

Illustrators: Gary Andrews and Shireen Nathoo Design

We are grateful to the following for permission to reproduce copyright material in the Learning Techniques section:
Tony Stone Images/David Young Wolff for photograph
Aerial Books and BBC publications for graph

MISTAKE	CORRECTION	NOTES

Learn from your mistakes **wf**

MISTAKE	CORRECTION	NOTES

MISTAKE	CORRECTION	NOTES

Review often and regularly

MISTAKE	CORRECTION	NOTES

SELF-CORRECTION

You can learn from your mistakes. Write your mistakes and the correct form in this Data system. This will help you to remember to use the correct form next time.

MISTAKE	CORRECTION	NOTES
Last night I went at a party.	Last night I went to a party.	Use to when the verb go has the idea of movement.
I have been to France two years ago.	I went to France two years ago.	Use the Past simple for something that happened at a specific time in the past.

Learn from your mistakes

IRREGULAR VERBS

INFINITIVE	PAST SIMPLE	PAST PARTICIPLE
know	knew	known
learn	learnt	learnt
leave	left	left
lend	lent	lent
let	let	let
lose	lost	lost
make	made	made
mean	meant	meant
meet	met	met
pay	paid	paid
put	put	put
read	read	read
ride	rode	ridden
ring	rang	rung
run	ran	run
say	said	said
see	saw	seen
sell	sold	sold
send	sent	sent
show	showed	shown
shut	shut	shut
sing	sang	sung
sit	sat	sat
sleep	slept	slept
speak	spoke	spoken
spell	spelt	spelt
spend	spent	spent
stand	stood	stood
steal	stole	stolen
swim	swam	swum
take	took	taken
teach	taught	taught
tear	tore	torn
tell	told	told
think	thought	thought
throw	threw	thrown
understand	understood	understood
wake up	woke up	woken up
wear	wore	worn
win	won	won
write	wrote	written

IRREGULAR VERBS

INFINITIVE	PAST SIMPLE	PAST PARTICIPLE
be	was/were	been
become	became	become
begin	began	begun
bite	bit	bitten
break	broke	broken
bring	brought	brought
build	built	built
buy	bought	bought
catch	caught	caught
choose	chose	chosen
come	came	come
cost	cost	cost
cut	cut	cut
do	did	done
drink	drank	drunk
drive	drove	driven
eat	ate	eaten
fall	fell	fallen
feel	felt	felt
find	found	found
fly	flew	flown
forget	forgot	forgotten
get	got	got
give	gave	given
go	went	gone
grow	grew	grown
have	had	had
hear	heard	heard
hit	hit	hit
hold	held	held
hurt	hurt	hurt
keep	kept	kept

GRAMMAR CHECK

- **Translate the following sentences into your language.**
- **Compare the structures in English and in your language. What is different? What is the same?**

1. The team practises every weekend. They are playing well at the moment.

   ....

2. A: I'm meeting her at 2.00.
   B: Are you going to get a taxi?
   A: No, I think I'll walk. It's not far.

   ....

   ....

   ....

3. I was having a shower when someone knocked on the door.

   ....

4. A: I went to New York last month. Have you ever been there?
   B: Yeah, I lived there for five years.

   ....

   ....

5. If I see Tom, I'll ask him to do it. *I'd* do it if I had more time.

   ....

6. I'll get three bottles of cola. Would you like some water too?

   ....

7. A: He drives really badly. He must be the worst driver I know.
   B: Yes, he *is* a bad driver. He should take some driving lessons!

   ....

   ....

DATAFLO

It could be you! — *advertisement for the National Lottery*

Write down any examples of *must/might/may/can't* you see or hear.

....

....

....

....

ABOUT ME

Complete these sentences so that they are true for you.

a .... can't be .... right now.

b .... might be .... at the moment.

c .... must be .... right now.

d I might .... sometime this week.

e I must .... today.

f I may .... sometime this year.

DATAPLUS

Now add more examples using *must/might/may/can't*.

....

....

....

You don't need to fill in all of Dataflo and Dataplus now. Write some examples and then come back and add more later.

MUST/MIGHT/MAY/CAN'T

It **must be** a house.
No, it **can't be**. Where's the door?

USE

Must/can't are used to make deductions. *Must* means you are very sure e.g. *He must be in his room.* (It is the only place that he can be.) *Might* and *may* mean that something is possible but that you are not sure e.g. *It might rain today. Can't* means that you are sure that something is not possible e.g. *They can't know where we are.*

FORM

PRESENT SIMPLE
Subject + *might* etc. + verb
POSITIVE
I/you/she/he/we/they **might** know John.
NEGATIVE
I/you/she/he/we/they **might not** know John.

⚠ Sometimes *could* is used with a similar meaning to *might/may* eg. *Someone's at the door. It could be Pete.*

DATAFLO

> You must write between 120 and 180 words for each question

from an exam paper

Write down any examples of *should/ought to/must/have to/don't have to* you see or hear.

....

....

....

ABOUT ME

Complete these sentences so that they are true for you.

a   I ought to .... but I never have the time.

b   I have to .... every day but I don't enjoy it.

c   I don't have to .... but I often do.

d   If you want to speak English well, I think you should ....
    ....

e   Something I must remember to do before the weekend is ....
    ....

DATAPLUS

Add more examples using *should/ought to/must/ have to/don't have to*.

....

....

....

> Choose a 'structure of the week'. Look and listen for it in books, newspapers, radio, TV, cinema etc. Use it as much as you can.

SHOULD/OUGHT TO/MUST/HAVE TO/DON'T HAVE TO

You **should go** to bed.

I **have to finish** this work before I go home.

You **don't have to come** shopping if you don't want to.

USE

1. *Should* and *ought* to have a similar meaning and are used to give advice.
2. *Have to* and *must* have a similar meaning and are used to express obligation i.e. there is no choice.
3. *Don't have to* means it is not necessary to do something.

FORM

Subject + *should* etc. + verb
POSITIVE I/you/she/he/we/they **should take** an aspirin.
NEGATIVE I/you/she/he/we/they **shouldn't take** an aspirin.
QUESTION **Should** I/you/she/he/we/they **take** an aspirin? Do I **have to take** an aspirin?

No smoking! =
You mustn't smoke NOT ~~You don't have to smoke~~.

DATAFLO

The <u>Best</u> of Simply Red   *from CD cover*

Write down any examples of comparative or superlative adjectives you see or hear.

....

....

....

ABOUT ME

Complete these sentences so that they are true for you.

a .... was one of the happiest times of my life.

b I am .... than I was a few years ago.

c The place where I was born is the most .... place I know.

d My best friend is .... than I am.

e .... is one of the best films I have ever seen.

DATAPLUS

Add more examples of your own using comparative or superlative adjectives.

....

....

....

Use your dictionary to check spelling

COMPARATIVES/SUPERLATIVES

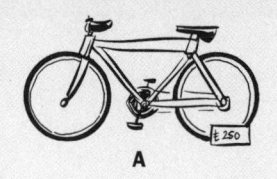

Bike A is more expensive than bike B but cheaper than bike C.
Bike B is the cheapest.
Bike C is the most expensive.

USE

We use comparative adjectives e.g. *cheaper* to compare two or more things.
We use superlative adjectives e.g. *the most expensive* to compare something with the rest of a particular group.

FORM

ADJECTIVE	COMPARATIVE	SUPERLATIVE
1a. cheap	cheaper (than)	(the) cheapest
1b. nice	nicer (than)	(the) nicest
1c. big	bigger (than)	(the) biggest
2a. modern	more modern (than)	(the) most modern
2b. funny	funnier (than)	(the) funniest
2c. expensive	more expensive (than)	(the) most expensive
3. good	better (than)	(the) best

1a. The comparative and superlative of one-syllable adjectives e.g. *cheap* are usually made by adding *-er* and (the) ... *-est*.
1b. When the adjective ends with an *-e* e.g. *nice*, you only add *-r* and *-st*.
1c. When the adjective ends with a vowel plus a consonant e.g. *big*, you double the consonant and add *-er* and *-est*.
2a. The comparative and superlative of two and three-syllable adjectives e.g. *modern*, is generally made by putting *more* or *(the) most* before the adjective.
2b. When a two-syllable adjective ends with *-y* e.g. *funny*, we make the comparative and superlative by replacing the *-y* with *-i* and adding *-er* or (the) ... *-est*.
2c. (See 2a above.)
3. Some adjectives have irregular comparative and superlative forms eg. *good–better–best; bad–worse–worst; far–further–furthest*

DATAFLO

I met this really interesting guy at Jo's party last night. We got on very well!

from a letter to a friend

Write down any examples of adverbs or adjectives you see or hear.

....

....

....

Complete these sentences so that they are true for you.

ABOUT ME

a   The last film I saw was really ....

because ....

b   I think Madonna sings ....

c   My father drives ....

d   The last time I was really surprised was ....

....

e   I work .... in the evening.

DATAPLUS

Add more examples using adverbs or adjectives.

....

....

....

Learn from your mistakes.
Use the **Self-correction Data system**.

ADVERBS/ADJECTIVES

1a He is a **bad** driver.
b He drives **badly**.

2a It was a **boring** film.
b We were **bored**.

USE

1. Adverbs tell us about the verb.
2. Adjectives tell us about the noun. In the example above, the *-ing* adjective tells us about the film. The *-ed* adjective tells us about how we felt about the film.

FORM

ADJECTIVE	ADVERB
1. slow	slowly
2. happy	happily
3. simple	simply
4. good	well
5. fast	fast
hard	hard

1. Adverbs which tell us about verbs are generally formed by adding -ly to the adjective.
2. If the adjective ends in *-y* we replace the *-y* with *-ily*.
3. If the adjective ends in *-le* we replace the *-e* with *-y*.
4 and 5. There are some irregular adverbs.

⚠ Not all words ending in *-ly* are adverbs. Some adjectives end in *-ly* too. For example: *friendly, lonely, silly, lovely*.
(Now look at **Word-building** for more information on suffixes.)

DATAFLO

> *We are having some fantastic weather. It's been sunny every day!*   from postcard

Write down any examples of countable or uncountable nouns you see or hear.

....

....

....

ABOUT ME

Complete these sentences so that they are true for you.

a   I've done .... work today.

b   We've had .... weather recently.

c   I never eat .... because ....

d   There's .... furniture in my bedroom and there are ....

e   The last time I did a lot of shopping for clothes was ....
    ....

DATAPLUS

Add more examples using countable or uncountable nouns.

....

....

....

You don't need to fill in all of Dataflo and Dataplus now.
Write some examples and then come back and add more later.

COUNTABLES/UNCOUNTABLES

Oh no! I've spilt **some cola** on the carpet.

Why did you buy **10 bottles of cola**?

USE

1. Uncountable nouns are things that cannot be counted eg. music, water etc. You can use *some* and *any* with uncountable nouns but we do not normally use *a/an*. *A little* and *much/a lot of* can also be used with uncountable nouns eg. *Could I have a little water, please? You haven't done much work today!*
2. Countable nouns are things that can be counted e.g. 5 minutes, 2 days, 3 bottles, 7 biscuits, 10 chairs etc. You can use *some* and *any* with plural countable nouns. *A few* and *many/a lot of* are also used with plural countable nouns e.g. *She's got a few interesting books. We don't see many people at weekends.*

FORM

COUNTABLES	UNCOUNTABLES
POSITIVE/NEGATIVE There is/isn't **a** book in my bag. There **are some/a lot of** books in my bag. There aren't **any** books in my bag.	POSITIVE/NEGATIVE I have **some/a lot of** information. I don't have **any/much/a lot of** information.
QUESTION Is there **a** book in my bag? Are there **any** books in your bag?	QUESTION Do you have **any** information?

⚠ A Some nouns can be countable or uncountable e.g.

1. *He's got black hair.*

2. *He's got a black hair.*

DATAFLO

> If you come to Barclays, you'll notice the difference!

from bank advertisement

Write down any examples of 1st or 2nd Conditional sentences you see or hear.

....

....

....

ABOUT ME

Complete these sentences so that they are true for you.

a   If I have time today, I'll ....

b   If I had £1 million, I would ....

c   If I could change one thing about my life, I'd ....

....

d   If I could visit any country in the world, I ....

because ....

e   If I learn to speak English well, I ....

f   My best friend would be happier if ....

DATAPLUS

Add more examples using the 1st or 2nd Conditional.

....

....

....

Highlight key parts of a new structure in colour to help you remember them eg. if I <u>had</u> more time, I <u>would paint</u> the kitchen.

1ST AND 2ND CONDITIONALS

If I see John, **I will give** him the book.

If I had enough money, **I would buy** a car.

USE

1. We use the 1st Conditional to show that something is a possibility i.e. in the example, it is possible but not certain that I will see John.
2. We use the 2nd Conditional to show that something is just imagination or probably will not happen i.e. in the example, the speaker does not have enough money to buy the car.

FORM

1ST CONDITIONAL *If* + Present simple, subject + *will* + verb	2ND CONDITIONAL *If* + Past simple, *would* + verb
If I/you/we/they **have** time, I/you/we/they**'ll clean** the bathroom.	**If** I/you/we/they **had** time, I/you/we/they**'d clean** the bathroom.
If she/he **has** time, she**'ll**/he**'ll clean** the bathroom.	**If** she/he **had** time, she/he**'d clean** the bathroom.

⚠ Notice that the form of the 2nd Conditional is the past but the meaning is not.

You can change the order of the clauses with these conditionals e.g. a) *If I had time, I'd clean the bathroom* and b) *I'd clean the bathroom if I had time* are both correct.

DATAFLO

> So, what have you done since you arrived in England?

from an informal conversation

Write down any examples of the Present perfect simple + *for/since* you see or hear.

....

....

....

ABOUT ME

Complete these sentences so that they are true for you or people you know.

a   I have .... for about .... years.

b   My parents have lived in .... since ....

c   .... has had the same job for ....

d   I have .... since I was very young.

e   We haven't .... for ages.

f   I haven't .... to my best friend since ....

DATAPLUS

Add more examples using the Present perfect simple + *for/since*.

....

....

....

You don't need to fill in all of Dataflo and Dataplus now. Write some examples now and then come back and add more later.

PRESENT PERFECT + *FOR/SINCE*

I've **lived** in Australia **since** 1995.

USE

One use of the Present perfect is to describe situations that have continued from some time in the past until now. We use *since* when we refer to a *point* of time in the past e.g. *We haven't seen him since the weekend.* We use *for* when we refer to a *period* of time e.g. *They've been married for more than 20 years.*

FORM

PRESENT PERFECT SIMPLE Subject + *have/has* + past participle	+ *for/since*
I/you/we/they **have lived** in America She/he/ **has lived** in America	**for** 2 weeks/6 months/3 years/ a long time. **since** March/1995/Sarah was born.

> ⚠ You can use both the Present perfect and the Past simple with *for*, but with different meanings e.g. a) *She's lived in London for about 2 years.* (she lives in London now) b) *She lived in London for about 2 years.* (she doesn't live in London now)

DATAFLO

> You have travelled all over the world but which is your favourite country?

from an interview with a famous journalist

Write down any examples of the Present perfect simple you see or hear.

....

....

....

ABOUT ME

Complete these sentences so that they are true for you.

a   I have been to .... different countries including ....

b   I have never .... and I don't want to!

c   .... is the best film I have ever ....

d   Not many people know that I have ....

e   There are many exciting things that I haven't done that I would like to do. For example: ....

DATAPLUS

Add more examples using the Present perfect simple.

....

....

....

PRESENT PERFECT/PAST SIMPLE

A **Have** you ever **been** to South America?
B Yes. I **went** to Brazil last year. It **was** fantastic!

USE

One use of the Present perfect simple is to describe something that happened in the past but without saying exactly when. This can be an example of personal experience e.g. *I've seen Michael Jackson in concert*.
We sometimes use *ever* (which means 'in your life') in the question form.
To find out or give more specific information we use the Past simple e.g. *When did you see him*?

FORM

PRESENT PERFECT SIMPLE Subject + *have/has*	+ past participle
POSITIVE/NEGATIVE I/you/we/they **have/have(n't)** She/he **has/has(n't)**	**eaten** snails.
QUESTION **Have** I/you/we/they (ever) **Has** she/he	**eaten** snails?

⚠ Regular past participles have the same *–ed* form as the Past simple e.g. *live–lived–lived*. But there are many irregular past participles e.g. *go–went–been*. (See Irregular verbs.)

DATAFLO

> Mike Maloney was having a drink when he heard a quiet voice in his ear.

from a detective novel

Write down any examples of the Past simple and Past continuous you see or hear.

....

....

....

ABOUT ME

Complete these sentences so that they are true for you.

a Yesterday I did a lot of different things. First I ...., then I ....

b Yesterday I was .... , when .... was ....
   (Use the Past continuous for actions that happen at the same time.)

c When I was going to work/school the other day, ... *(Describe things that happened).*

d Someone telephoned me when I was ....

e Last year my best friend was .... , when I was ....

DATAPLUS

Add more examples using the Past simple and Past continuous.

....

....

....

Add a note to your examples to say if they are formal or informal, written or spoken English.

PAST SIMPLE/PAST CONTINUOUS

I **was having** a shower yesterday when someone **knocked** on the door.

USE

1. One use of the Past continuous is to describe an action that is 'interrupted' by another action (expressed by the Past simple).
2. Another use of the Past continuous is to describe actions that happened at the same time e.g. *When I was cleaning the house, Judith was having coffee with her friends.*
3. The Past simple is used to describe an action which happened in the past and has finished. We generally know when it finished.

FORM

PAST CONTINUOUS Subject + *was/were* + verb *-ing*		PAST SIMPLE (regular verbs) Subject + verb *-ed*	
POSITIVE/NEGATIVE I/she/he **was** You/we/they **were**	**(not) watching** TV.	POSITIVE/NEGATIVE I/you/she/he/we/they	**called.** **didn't call.**
QUESTION **Was** I/she/he **Were** you/we/they	**watching** TV.	QUESTION **Did** I/you/she/he/we/they **call**?	

> Be careful about the pronunciation of regular Past simple forms e.g. asked /t/, lived /d/, wanted /ɪd/
>
> There are many verbs with an irregular Past simple form – see **Irregular verbs** at the end of this section.
>
> There are some verbs e.g. *know, want, believe* that are not normally used in the continuous.

DATAFLO

We're visiting the Eiffel Tower tomorrow morning! *(from a postcard)*

Write down any examples of the Present continuous (with future meaning), *going to* or *will* you see or hear.

....

....

....

ABOUT ME

Complete these sentences so that they are true for you.

a   This weekend I am ....
    (Describe any arrangements you have made).

b   Next year I am going to ....

c   I think .... win the next election in my country.

d   I think my best friend will .... next year.

e   The next time I am going out with friends is ....
    .... We ....
    (Describe what you plan/or have arranged to do).

DATAPLUS

Add more examples using the Present continuous (with future meaning), *going to* or *will*.

....

....

....

You can compare grammar structures in English and in your language.
e.g. *I am going to wash my hands > Je vais me laver les mains.*

GOING TO/WILL/ PRESENT CONTINUOUS (FUTURE)

1 I **am taking** Jenny to the theatre on her birthday. (I've bought the tickets.)

2a I **am going to buy** Jenny some earrings for her birthday.

2b OK. Then, I'**ll get** her some CDs.

USE

1. One use of the Present continuous is to describe future arrangements.

2a. One use of the 'going to' future is to express future plans. We also use it to make a prediction when you have some evidence eg. *It's going to rain.* (I can see the black clouds in the sky.)

2b. One use of 'will' is to express decisions that we make at the time of speaking. It is also used to make predictions e.g. *I think he'll arrive early.*

FORM

For the Present continuous form see previous pages.

GOING TO Subject + *am/is/are* + *going to* + infinitive		WILL Subject + *will* + infinitive
POSITIVE/NEGATIVE I **am** You/we/they **are** She/he/it **is**	(not) going to visit Tom tomorrow.	POSITIVE/NEGATIVE I/you/he/she/it/we/they'**ll visit** Tom tomorrow
QUESTION **Am** I **Are** you **Is** she/he	going to visit Tom tomorrow?	QUESTION **Shall** I/we **visit** Tom tomorrow?

⚠ 'Going to' and the Present continuous are more common ways of expressing the future than 'will'. 'Will' can be used to express offers, promises, e.g. *I'll help you with your homework.* (promise) We usually only use 'shall' with *I* or *we* to make suggestions or offers e.g. *Shall I open the door for you?* (offer)

DATAFLO

> Americans usually take two weeks holiday a year.

from a tourist guide book

Write down any examples of the Present simple or Present continuous you see or hear.

....

....

....

ABOUT ME

Complete these sentences so that they are true for you.

a   I always .... at the weekend.

b   My best friend and I sometimes ....

c   Right now, my best friend is probably ....

d   I never .... but I should!

e   I am .... at the moment, but that will soon change.

DATAPLUS

Add more examples using the Present simple or Present continuous.

....

....

....

You don't need to fill in all of Dataflo and Dataplus now.
Write some examples and then come back and add more later.

PRESENT SIMPLE/PRESENT CONTINUOUS

PRESENT SIMPLE
They always **play** basketball at the weekend.

PRESENT CONTINUOUS
They **are playing** basketball with their friends.

ADVERBS OF FREQUENCY

0%			50%			100%
never	occasionally	sometimes		often	usually	always

USE

1. One use of the Present simple is to describe things we do regularly. We often use it with adverbs of frequency.
   We also use it for things which are always true e.g. *I come from London.*

2. One use of the Present continuous is to describe an action which is happening now.
   It is also used to describe temporary situations e.g. *I am staying with friends.*

FORM

PRESENT SIMPLE Subject + verb (+*s/es*)	PRESENT CONTINUOUS Subject + *am/is/are* + verb + *-ing*
POSITIVE/NEGATIVE I/you/we/they **(don't) work**. She/he/it **works**. 　　　**doesn't work**.	POSITIVE/NEGATIVE I **am**　　　　　　　　| **(not) working**. You/we/they **are** She/he/it **is**
QUESTION **Do** I/you/we/they | **work**? **Does** she/he/it	QUESTION **Am** I **Are** you/we/they　| **working**? **Is** she/he/it

⚠ Don't forget to add '*s*' or '*es*' to the Present simple 3rd person singular e.g. *She play**s** tennis. She watch**es** a lot of TV.* Add '*es*' to verbs ending in 'ch', 'o', 'sh', 'ss' and 'x'.

You can write sentences about yourself using the structures you are practising.	**About Me, Dataplus** in the Grammar section.
You can compare grammar structures in English and in your language. What is different? What is the same?	*I am going to wash my hands. Je vais me laver les mains.*
You can use the answer key to grammar exercises to help you understand the grammar rules while you do the exercises.	Grammar practice books.
Learn from your mistakes.	**Self-correction** pages.
Choose a 'structure of the week'. Look and listen for it. Use it as much as you can.	Books, newspapers, magazines, radio, TV, cinema etc.

GRAMMAR STRATEGIES

Look at the following grammar strategies.

- **Which ones do you use? Why?**
- **Which new ones will you try? Why?**
- **Find examples of the strategies in the Grammar section to see how to use them.**

Strategy	Example
You can write down examples of grammar structures.	**Dataflo** in the Grammar Section.
You can check your examples by looking at grammar explanations.	**Use** in the Grammar section.
Memorise irregular forms.	**Irregular verbs**
You can mark changes in form with coloured pens.	I like Chinese food. He likes Chinese food.
Look for patterns and write your own sentences.	What do you think? *What do you want?* *What do you like?*

GRAMMAR

CONTENTS

Grammar strategies

Present simple (+ adverbs of frequency)/Present continuous

Going to/Will/Present continuous (future)

Past simple/Past continuous

Present perfect/Past simple

Present perfect + *for/since*

Conditionals (1st and 2nd)

Countables/Uncountables

Adverbs/Adjectives (*-ing* v. *-ed*)

Comparatives/Superlatives

Should/ought to/must/have to/don't have to

Must/might/may/can't

Irregular verbs

Photocopiable

Photocopiable

Review often and regularly

Photocopiable

Use these pages for situations which are useful for you.

Photocopiable

You can come back and add more later

In class

How do you spell ......?
How do you pronounce ......?
Where's the stress in this word?
What does ...... mean?
Excuse me, I don't understand.
I'm sorry, I don't understand.
Could you say that again, please?
Why are we doing this, please?
Could you explain again, please?
Where can I find ......?
Can you look at this, please?
I've got a problem with ......
Can you help me, please?
Can we do this again, please?
What are we doing next lesson?
Excuse me, can we stop now, please? I would like to review.

Letters

Dear John ..... Lots of love / Best wishes / All the best **(informal)**

Dear Mr. Brown ..... Yours sincerely **(formal)**

Dear Sir/Madam ..... Yours faithfully **(formal)**

I'm looking forward to hearing from you. **(informal)**

I look forward to hearing from you. **(formal)**

Write down phrases which are important to you

Good News / Bad News

For something new (a new job; a baby; someone is going to get married): Congratulations! / That's wonderful news! / I'm so happy for you! / That's great!

For birthdays: Happy birthday!

Passing an exam: Well done!

When someone is not well: Poor you! / You poor thing! / Oh, I am sorry.

When something bad happens: I'm so sorry. Is there anything I can do?

USEFUL PHRASES

- Are there situations in which you *often* use English, for example, on the telephone, responding to good or bad news, writing a letter in class?

- On the following pages you will find examples of language which are useful in these situations.

- Add new useful phrases to these pages when you learn them, and use the blank pages for other situations that are important for you.

Telephoning

A Could I speak to Marie, please?
B Speaking.
A This is Carlos.
B Hang on. *(informal)*
A Could you hold on a moment, please? *(more formal)*

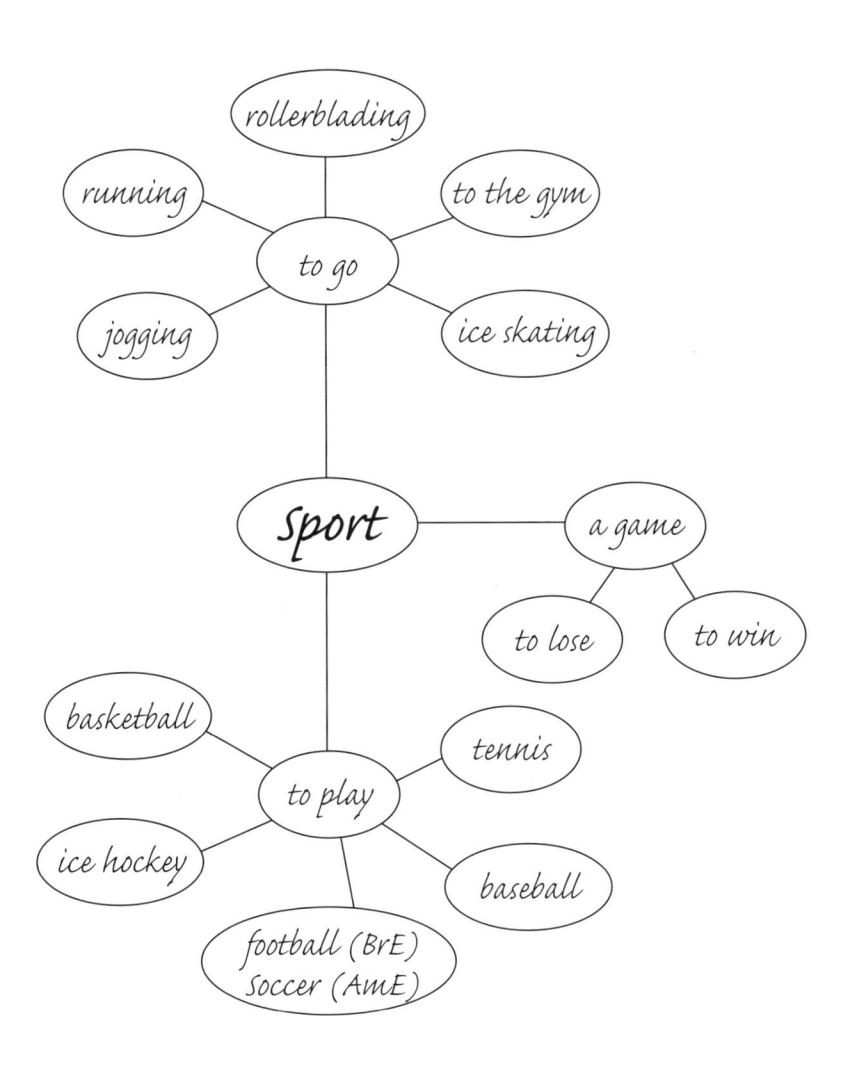

- **sport**
  - **to go**
    - rollerblading
    - running
    - jogging
    - to the gym
    - ice skating
  - **a game**
    - to lose
    - to win
  - **to play**
    - basketball
    - ice hockey
    - tennis
    - baseball
    - football (BrE) / soccer (AmE)

KEY

A-Z possible answers (your answers may be a little different)

Q R	WORD/EXPRESSION PRONUNCIATION	PART OF SPEECH	PICTURE, MEANING OR TRANSLATION	EXAMPLE SENTENCE	NOTES
	to have a row /aʊ/	expr.	to have an angry argument	My sister had a terrible row with her boyfriend last night.	have a row <u>about</u> something.

S T	WORD/EXPRESSION PRONUNCIATION	PART OF SPEECH	PICTURE, MEANING OR TRANSLATION	EXAMPLE SENTENCE	NOTES
	stomach-ache	n.	pain in your stomach	I ate too much last night, and now I have a stomach-ache.	headache backache toothache

TOPICS
Word webs

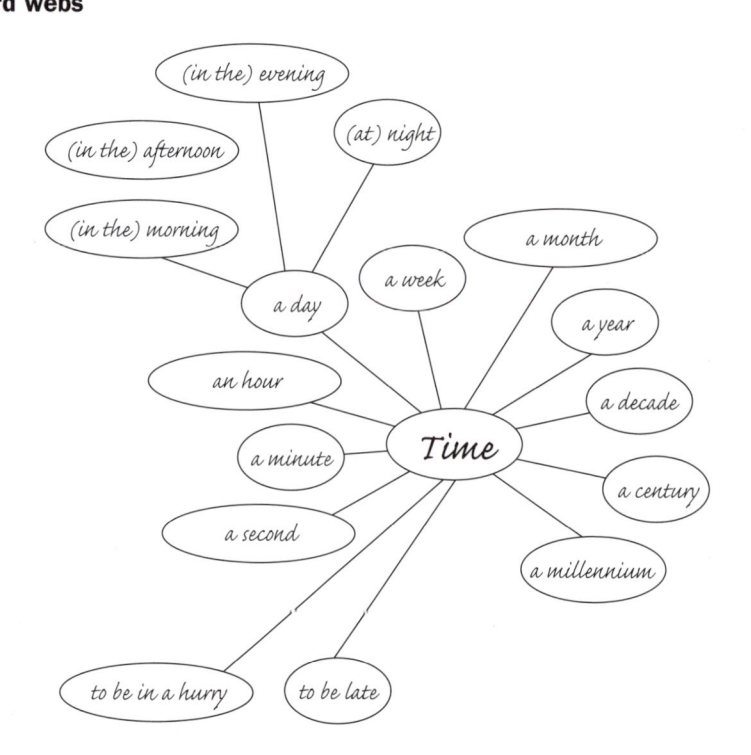

- Time
  - a day
    - (in the) evening
    - (at) night
    - (in the) afternoon
    - (in the) morning
  - a week
  - a month
  - a year
  - a decade
  - a century
  - a millennium
  - an hour
  - a minute
  - a second
  - to be in a hurry
  - to be late

	dictionary obviously	intelligent advertisement	population understanding	unfortunately	university international	communication

STRESS PATTERNS

Use this Data system to help you remember where the stress is in a word.

● ● ●	engineer Japanese
● ● ● ●	unhappy informal
● ● ● ●	telephone beautiful
● ●	goodbye fifteen
● ●	doctor chocolate

Photocopiable

The stressed syllable is usually longer and louder than the other syllables

SOMETHING TO TRY

Check your answers in your dictionary or in the key at the end of this section. Use a good dictionary like the *Longman Active Study Dictionary*.

1. **Choice of words**

   Use your dictionary to find out how many meanings these words have:

   tight   party
   record permit

2. **Parts of speech**

   What parts of speech do these words have? Do some of them have more than one?

   computer judge
   interest   fly

3. **Prepositions**

   Fill in the missing prepositions:

   I want to talk .... you.

   She's very good .... English.

   I'm waiting .... Sue to arrive.

4. **Stress patterns**

   The stress marks in your dictionary tell you which part of a word to say strongly. For example, /ˌælfəˈbetɪkəl/ means we say *alphabétical*.

   Put a circle around the correct stress patterns:

   táble | tablé
   sitúation | situátion
   húrry | hurrý
   récord (v) | recórd (v)

5. **Opposites**

   Use your dictionary to find out the opposites of these words:

   kind (adj)   clockwise
   disadvantage honest

6. **Phrasal verbs**

   Use your dictionary to put the correct phrasal verb in these sentences. Look up the phrasal verb under the main verb in italics:

   She's trying to .... smoking. [*give*]

   What time do you .... in the morning [*get*]

   I had to walk to work today because my car .... [*break*]

Sound/pronunciation

sound	**fifteen** /fɪfˈtiːn/ *det, n. pron* the number	This tells you how to pronounce a word.
stress	**apple** /ˈæpəl/ n **1.** a hard round fruit with juicy flesh and red, green, or yellow skin	This mark tells you which part of a word to say strongly. The first syllable of <u>apple</u> is stressed.
NOTE: This dictionary uses ' to mark stress. *Wordflo* uses •, i.e. <u>i•ncrease</u>/<u>incre•ase</u>	**increase** /ɪnˈkriːs/ v **1.** to become larger in amount, number, or degree **increase** /ˈɪŋkriːs/ n **1.** a rise in amount, number, or degree	When words have two or more syllables, one is always stressed more strongly. This tells you that the verb <u>increase</u> and the noun <u>increase</u> are stressed differently. ▶ Stress patterns

Grammar

parts of speech	**age** /eɪdʒ/ n **1.** the number of years a person has lived **age** /eɪdʒ/ v **aged, aging,** or **ageing** [I,T] to become older and weaker, or to make someone seem older and weaker	The letters tell you whether a word is a verb, a noun, an adjective or an adverb. ▶ A–Z
word families	**cook** /kʊk/ v [I,T] to prepare food for eating using heat **cooking** n [U]	You can often form more words from the word you know. This tells you that the noun form of the verb <u>cook</u> is <u>cooking</u>. ▶ Word-builder
phrasal verbs	**drop** /drɒp/ v **1.** to let something fall unintentionally, accidentally, or suddenly: *He dropped the ball and ran.* **drop in** *phr v* [I] to visit someone unexpectedly or informally: *I'll drop in some time next week.*	Some verbs combine with other words to form <u>phrasal verbs</u> which have their own meaning. They are listed in alphabetical order after the main verb. ▶ Phrasal verbs
words that go with other words	**crime** /kraɪm/ n **1.** [C] an action which is punishable by law: *Drug smuggling is a serious crime.*| *She committed a terrible crime.*	The examples show you that some words are typically used with other words, i.e. <u>serious</u> crime/<u>commit</u> a crime. ▶ Word partners
verbs followed by prepositions	**escape** /ɪˈskeɪp/ v **escaped, escaping** **1.** to succeed in getting out of a place where you are kept by force: *They escaped from prison.*	This tells you what prepositions to use after a verb. ▶ A–Z

WHAT YOUR DICTIONARY TELLS YOU

Spelling

British and American spellings

> **colour** /ˈkʌləʳ/ *n* (**color** *AmE*) **1.** the quality which allows you to see the difference between, for example, a red flower and a blue flower when they are both the same size and shape.

American spellings are shown in brackets like this.

Meaning

definitions

examples

> **study** /ˈstʌdi/ *v* **studied, studying:** **1.** to spend time learning a subject: *He studies French.| He's studying to be a doctor.* **2.** to examine something carefully: *Before leaving they studied the map.| Jack studied her face closely.*

This tells you what a word means.

This tells you how the word is used in natural English.

▶ A–Z, Phrasal verbs, Power verbs

words with more than one meaning

> **match** /mætʃ/ *n* **1.** [C] a short thin stick of wood that produces a flame when it is struck against a rough surface: *a box of matches* **2.** [C] a game or sports event: *a football match| a chess match* **3.** [sing] a thing that is like another thing or suitable for use with something: *The hat and shoes are a perfect match.*

Many words have more than one meaning. This tells you that the noun match has three meanings. The most common meaning is first.

opposites

> **happy** /ˈhæpi/ *adj* **happier happiest** **1.** feeling, expresssing, or giving pleasure and satisfaction: *a happy child | You look very happy.| a happy marriage| I'm not very happy about their decision.*
> -opposite **unhappy**

This tells you what the opposite of a word is.

▶ A–Z, Topic pages

choosing the right word

> **kid** /kɪd/ *n* [C] **1.** *infml* a child or young person: *My kids are two and six.| college kids| It's immoral putting kids in uniform and sending them to fight a war.*

This shows you that kid is informal, so you would not use it in formal writing.

The extracts are taken from the *Longman Active Study Dictionary*.

Photocopiable

© Addison Wesley Longman Limited 1998

Wordflo

DICTIONARY TIPS

You can use your dictionary in many ways to help you with your English.

USE YOUR DICTIONARY TO:

Find the **meaning** of a word or phrase in clear English.

Check the **spelling** of a word.

Find out if a word or spelling is **British** or **American**, because these are sometimes different.

Find the correct **pronunciation** of a word, with its **stress pattern**.

Find **examples** of how a word is typically used. This helps you to understand the word in context, and also how to use that word yourself.

Find out about the **grammar** of a word.

Find out what words typically **appear with other words**.

Use a good dictionary like the Longman Active Study Dictionary

INFO

WORD PRONUNCIATION

WORDS WITH THE SAME PRONUNCIATION		
by	buy	bye
check	cheque	
four	for	
hear	here	
I	eye	
meet	meat	
no	know	
nose	knows	
one	won	
piece	peace	
red	read	
sea	see	
son	sun	
there	their	
through	threw	
two	too	to
wait	weight	
way	weigh	
where	wear	
write	right	

INFO

PRONUNCIATION TABLE

CONSONANTS			VOWELS	
Phonetic Symbol	Keyword		Phonetic Symbol	Keyword
p	**p**en		ɪ	b**i**t
b	**b**ack		e	b**e**d
t	**t**en		æ	c**a**t
d	**d**ay	short	ɒ	d**o**g (BrE)
k	**k**ey		ʌ	b**u**t
g	**g**et		ʊ	p**u**t
f	**f**ast		ə	**a**bout
v	**v**iew		i	happ**y**
θ	**th**ing		iː	sh**ee**p
ð	**th**en		ɑː	f**a**ther
s	**s**oon		ɒː	d**o**g (AmE)
z	**z**ero		ɔː	f**ou**r
ʃ	**sh**ip		uː	b**oo**t
ʒ	plea**s**ure		ɜː	b**ir**d
tʃ	**ch**ild		eɪ	m**a**ke
dʒ	**j**ump		aɪ	l**i**fe
m	**m**an	long	ɔɪ	b**oy**
n	**n**ame		əʊ	n**o**te (BrE)
ŋ	si**ng**		oʊ	n**o**te (AmE)
w	**w**et		aʊ	n**ow**
l	**l**et		ɪə	r**ea**l
r	**r**ed		eə	h**air**
j	**y**et		ʊə	s**ure**
			uə	us**ua**l
			iə	happ**ier**

NOTES

NOTES

NOTES

NOTES

NOTES

NOTES

NOTES

NOTES

Photocopiable

Write down the Word partners of other common words when you learn them.

→ *work*　　NOTES

work ←　　NOTES

→ *good*　　NOTES

good ←　　NOTES

Look for other Word partners when you read

- **Look at the words next to the arrows below.**

- **Then look at the words in this list.**
  club   trip   and night   life   and day   dream

- **Write the words in the correct arrows below.**
  Write notes when they are useful.

- **Check your answers in the key at the end of Dicitonary skills.**

day
- ...off...
- ....
- ....
- ....

NOTES

night
- ...out...
- ....
- ....
- ....

NOTES

WORD PARTNERS

Some words are often used together. They are Word partners.

- Look at the words in and next to the arrows below.

- Look at the words in this list:
  be in   limit   table   spare

- They can all go with the word time. Some go before it and some go after it.

- Write the words in the correct boxes below.

- You can write notes, for example, meaning, example sentence, stress.

- Check your answers in the key at the end of Dictionary skills.

..part..
a good

> *time*

NOTES

time <

-consuming

NOTES

You can come back and add more later

EXAMPLE SENTENCE	MEANING/TRANSLATION

Photocopiable

go

EXAMPLE SENTENCE	MEANING/TRANSLATION

give

EXAMPLE SENTENCE	MEANING/TRANSLATION

Photocopiable

turn

EXAMPLE SENTENCE	MEANING/TRANSLATION

take

EXAMPLE SENTENCE	MEANING/TRANSLATION

Photocopiable

put

EXAMPLE SENTENCE	MEANING/TRANSLATION

- **Look at the expressions made with the Power verb** get.

- **Write an example sentence and the meaning or translation for each of the expressions.**

- **Think of other expressions with** get. **Add them to the star and write an example sentence and the meaning or translation for each one.**

get

to get a new car/a CD player

to get angry/ hungry/ tired

EXAMPLE SENTENCE	MEANING/TRANSLATION

- **Look at the expressions, example sentences and meanings made with the Power verb do.**

- **Think of other expressions with do. Add them to the star.**

- **Write an example sentence and the meaning or translation for each of the expressions you write.**

What do you do? *to do an English course*

do

to do well/badly

EXAMPLE SENTENCE	MEANING/TRANSLATION
What does your sister do?	What's her job?
I'm doing a course to improve my English.	I'm taking a course.
He did well at school.	He was very successful.

Use your dictionary to check spelling and pronunciation

- **Look at the expressions you can use with the Power verb** make.
- **Look at the example sentences and the meanings in the chart below.**
- **Write another example sentence for each of the expressions.**

make someone angry/happy/sad

make

to make a mistake/mistakes

made of silk/cotton etc.

EXAMPLE SENTENCE	MEANING/TRANSLATION
He really *makes me angry* sometimes!	I sometimes get very angry with him.
When I'm tired, I *make a lot of mistakes* at work.	I do a lot of things wrong.
What's your bag *made of*?	What material is your bag?

POWER VERBS

'Power verbs' are very common and useful verbs that can be part of many expressions. Use this Data system to write them down.

- **Look at the expressions on the star you can use with the Power verb** have. **Look at the example sentences and meanings in the chart.**

- **Write in the meanings or translations for** to have lunch **and** to have time.

- **Check your answers in the key at the end of Dictionary skills.**

Star (have):
- to have breakfast/lunch/dinner/a meal
- to have a shower/bath
- to have a headache/stomach-ache/sore throat etc.
- to have time (to do something)

EXAMPLE SENTENCE	MEANING/TRANSLATION
Have you got any aspirin? I have a terrible headache.	I have a very bad pain in my head.
What time did you have lunch?	
I didn't have time to go to the shops.	

Remember to add to and renew your **Data systems**

EXAMPLE SENTENCE	MEANING/TRANSLATION

EXAMPLE SENTENCE	MEANING/TRANSLATION

EXAMPLE SENTENCE	MEANING/TRANSLATION

bring

EXAMPLE SENTENCE	MEANING/TRANSLATION

make

EXAMPLE SENTENCE	MEANING/TRANSLATION

You can now write phrasal verbs with take, make, bring **and many other common verbs.**

take

EXAMPLE SENTENCE	MEANING/TRANSLATION

Photocopiable

Write example sentences about your life and interests

- **Look at the phrasal verbs with** get **and the example sentences and meanings in the chart.**

- **Write the meaning/translation and an example sentence for** get up.

- **Check your answers in the key at the end of Dictionary skills.**

get ..over..
..on with..
..up..

EXAMPLE SENTENCE	MEANING/TRANSLATION
I've had flu, but I'm getting over it now.	to get well again after an illness
Do you get on with your teacher?	to have a good relationship with someone

PHRASAL VERBS

Phrasal verbs are verbs that have two or three parts. You can write them in this Datasystem.

- Look at the phrasal verbs with put and the example sentences and meanings in the chart.
- Write the meaning or translation for put off.
- Check your answers in the key at the end of Dictionary skills.

Put .out...... .on...... .off......

EXAMPLE SENTENCE	MEANING/TRANSLATION
It took them three hours to <u>put out</u> the fire.	to stop a fire from burning
He got up and <u>put on</u> his coat.	to put clothes on your body
We had to <u>put off</u> the meeting until the following weekend.	

You can come back and add more later

- **Look at the words and expressions below. Add them to the Word web.**
  ice-skating
  to win
  baseball
  tennis

- **Then compare your Word web with the one in the key at the end of Dictionary skills.**

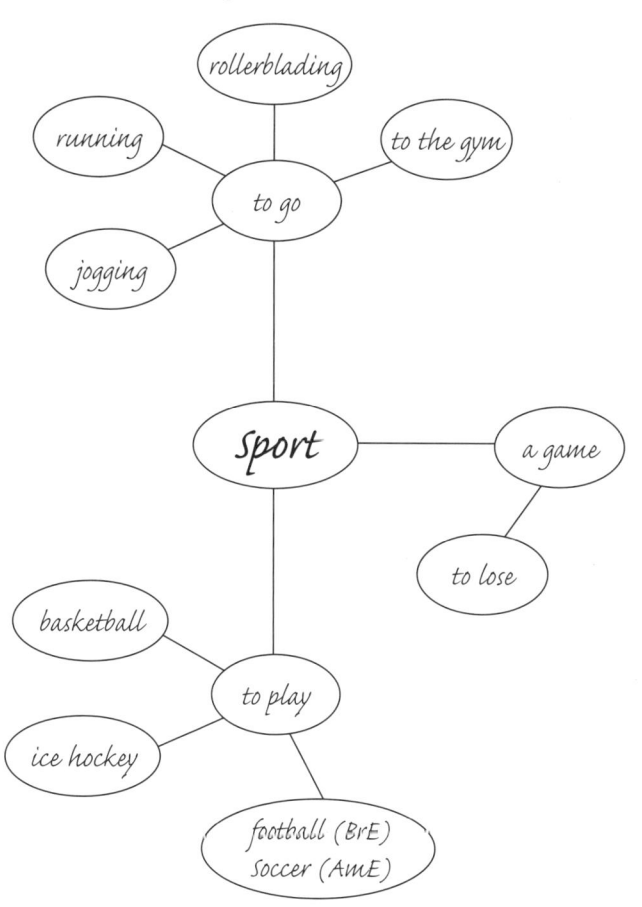

```
           rollerblading
running                  to the gym
           to go
jogging


              sport ─── a game
             /       \
            /         to lose
       to play
       /  |  \
basketball |  football (BrE)
ice hockey    Soccer (AmE)
```

WORD WEB

In the Word webs Data system you can show connections between many words and expressions.

- Look at the centre of the Word web below. What is the topic?

- Look at these words and expressions. Write them in the best places in the Word web.
  a month
  (in the) evening
  an hour
  a second

- Then check your answers in the key at the end of Dictionary skills.

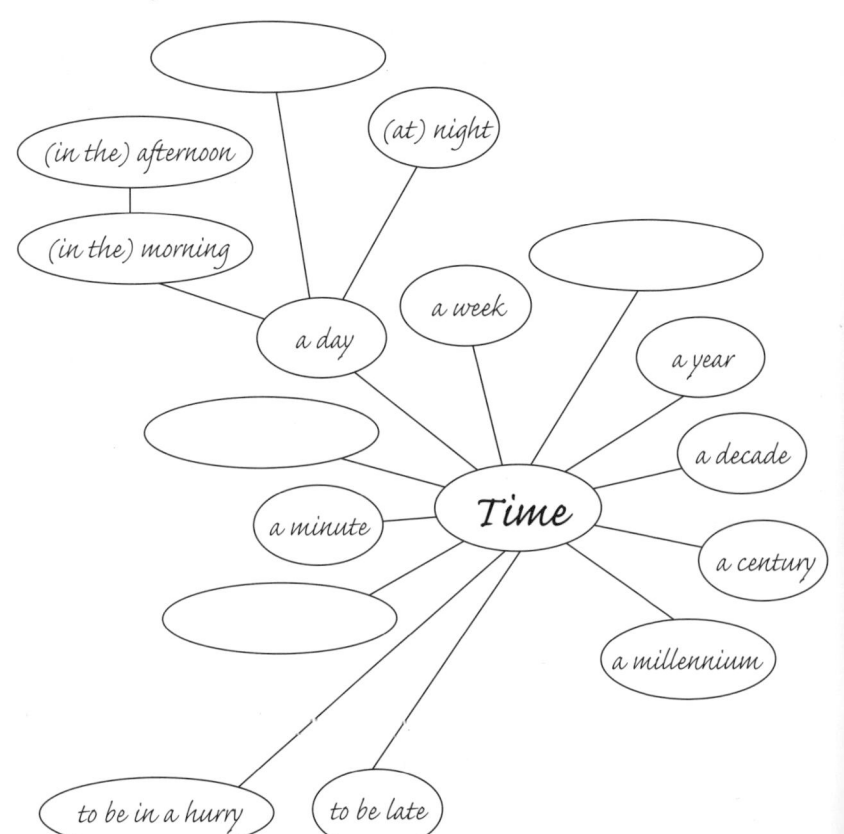

(in the) afternoon — *(in the) morning* — *a day*
(at) night
a week
a minute
Time
a year
a decade
a century
a millennium
to be in a hurry
to be late

You can come back and add more later

	VERB
	NOUN
	PERSON
	ADJECTIVE
	ADVERB

Photocopiable

VERB	NOUN	PERSON	ADJECTIVE	ADVERB

Use your dictionary to check spelling and pronunciation

Now build words in the Word-builder.

	VERB
	NOUN
	PERSON
	ADJECTIVE
	ADVERB

WORD-BUILDER

Use the Word-builder Data system to make more words from the words you already know.

- **Look at the examples in the chart.**

- **Now complete the chart with the following:**
  create   interesting

- **Check in the key at the end of Dictionary skills.**

VERB	NOUN	PERSON	ADJECTIVE	ADVERB
to use /z/	use /s/	• user /z/	• useful /s/ • useless /s/	• usefully /s/ • uselessly /s/
to cook /ʊ/	• cooking /ʊ/ • cooker /ʊ/ (kitchen appliance)	cook /ʊ/ (job)	cooked /t/ uncooked /t/ undercooked overcooked	

You can also write these words in the **A–Z** and add an example sentence

SUFFIXES

A suffix is a group of letters at the end of some words. It often tells us if the word is a noun, verb, adjective or adverb. For example, in the word information, -ation **tells you the word is a noun.**

NOUN SUFFIX	EXAMPLE WORDS
-ment	improvement
-ation	information
-tion	production
-ion	expression
-er	writer
-ness	happiness
VERB SUFFIX	EXAMPLE WORDS
-ify	identify
-ate	communicate
-ise	emphasise
-en	strengthen
ADJECTIVE SUFFIX	EXAMPLE WORDS
-ial	financial
-ful	careful
-less	careless
-ate	accurate
-able	capable
-ive	active
ADVERB SUFFIX	EXAMPLE WORDS
-ly	carefully

PREFIXES

A prefix is a group of letters added to the beginning of a word to change its meaning. For example, smoking and non-smoking (non **is a prefix**).

PREFIX	MEANING	EXAMPLE WORDS
anti-	against	anti-American
co-	with, together, equally	cooperate
dis-	not, opposite	disappear
im-	not, opposite	impossible
in-	not, opposite	independent
mis-	wrongly	misspell
non-	not, opposite	non-fiction
over-	too much	overcooked
pro-	for, in favour of	pro-American
re-	again, back	rebuild
un-	not, opposite	uncertain
under-	too little	undercooked

Photocopiable

Photocopiable

Write about topics that are important to you

- Look at this Topic page on food.
- Write some words and expressions under the heading Fruit.

Food

Vegetables
carrots
peas

red
green } pepper
yellow

Meat
chicken — fried chicken
chicken — roast chicken

from a cow — roast beef
from a cow — hamburger
steak

I'd like my steak/hamburger
rare ↑ (less cooked)
medium
well done ↓ (more cooked)

Adjectives
spicy
HOT! HOT!
(Mexican food is spicy)

sour
sauə^r
(lemons are sour)

bitter
(coffee is bitter without sugar)

sweet
to have a sweet tooth
(to like sweet things a lot)

Fruit
....
....
....
....
....

TOPIC PAGES

You can keep all the words about a particular topic in this Data system.

- Look at this Topic page on music.
- Add more words in the blanks.

Music

Types of music
classical (NOT classic)
rock
....
....

People
musician
singer
guitarist or guitar player
....
....

Instruments
guitar
saxophone (also sax.)

drum

drumsticks

....
....

loud ←(opposite)→ soft
music

to play the | piano
            | drums
            | etc.

to listen to music
NOT to ~~listen music~~
_____

to play | a CD = compact disc
put on | a ....
take off |
listen to |

Draw pictures to help you remember the meanings of words and expressions

Photocopiable

Wordflo © Addison Wesley Longman Limited 1998

Photocopiable

Add pronunciation where you think it is useful

Now create your own Word webs with vocabulary that is important for you.

- **Look at the words and expressions below. Add them to the Word web.**

  teenager/adolescent
  old/elderly (man/woman)
  middle-aged (man/woman)
  young (man/woman)
  beautiful (woman)
  toddler

  average
  child
  baby
  good-looking
  ugly

- **Compare your Word web with the one in the key at the end of Dictionary skills.**

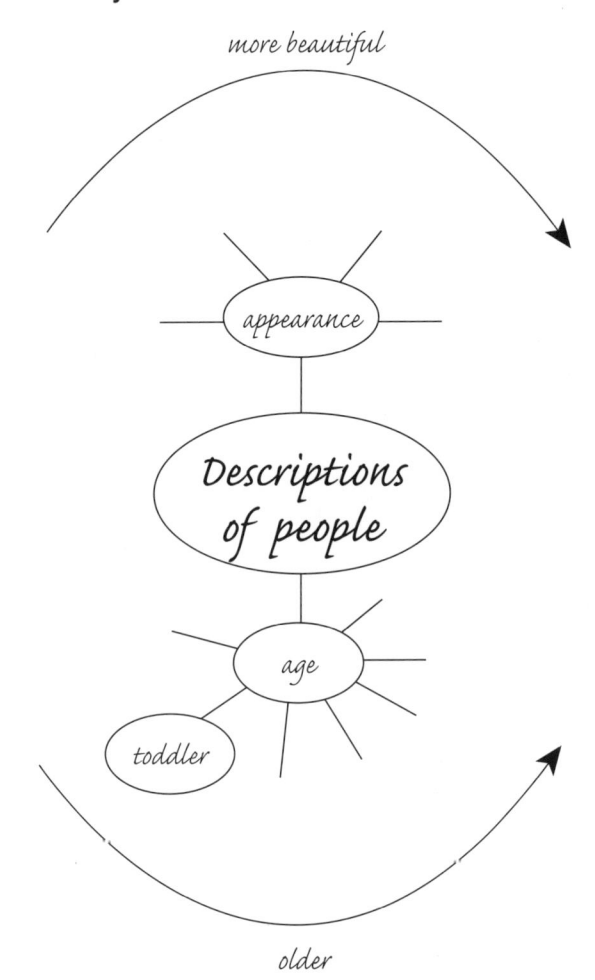

more beautiful

appearance

Descriptions of people

age

toddler

older

Learning vocabulary is easy when you have a system

WORD/EXPRESSION PRONUNCIATION	PART OF SPEECH	PICTURE, MEANING OR TRANSLATION	EXAMPLE SENTENCE	NOTES

Photocopiable

WORD/EXPRESSION PRONUNCIATION	PART OF SPEECH	PICTURE, MEANING OR TRANSLATION	EXAMPLE SENTENCE	NOTES
weak /iː/	adj.	not strong	When I had flu I felt very <u>weak</u>.	weak person weak tea

WORD/EXPRESSION PRONUNCIATION	PART OF SPEECH	PICTURE, MEANING OR TRANSLATION	EXAMPLE SENTENCE	NOTES

Photocopiable

WORD/EXPRESSION PRONUNCIATION	PART OF SPEECH	PICTURE, MEANING OR TRANSLATION	EXAMPLE SENTENCE	NOTES
to turn on /ɜːl/	phrasal verb	OFF ⊙ ON To make something electrical or a machine start working.	Could you turn on the light, please?	opposite: to turn off. to turn on/off = to switch on/off

Photocopiable

You can write opposites in the Notes column

WORD/EXPRESSION PRONUNCIATION	PART OF SPEECH	PICTURE, MEANING OR TRANSLATION	EXAMPLE SENTENCE	NOTES

Photocopiable

WORD/EXPRESSION PRONUNCIATION	PART OF SPEECH	PICTURE, MEANING OR TRANSLATION	EXAMPLE SENTENCE	NOTES

Write example sentences about your life and interests

WORD/EXPRESSION PRONUNCIATION	PART OF SPEECH	PICTURE, MEANING OR TRANSLATION	EXAMPLE SENTENCE	NOTES

WORD/EXPRESSION PRONUNCIATION	PART OF SPEECH	PICTURE, MEANING OR TRANSLATION	EXAMPLE SENTENCE	NOTES

WORD/EXPRESSION PRONUNCIATION	PART OF SPEECH	PICTURE, MEANING OR TRANSLATION	EXAMPLE SENTENCE	NOTES

Photocopiable

© Addison Wesley Longman Limited 1998

Wordflo

WORD/EXPRESSION PRONUNCIATION	PART OF SPEECH	PICTURE, MEANING OR TRANSLATION	EXAMPLE SENTENCE	NOTES

Photocopiable

Does your word/expression start with G or H?

WORD/EXPRESSION PRONUNCIATION	PART OF SPEECH	PICTURE, MEANING OR TRANSLATION	EXAMPLE SENTENCE	NOTES

Photocopiable

WORD/EXPRESSION PRONUNCIATION	PART OF SPEECH	PICTURE, MEANING OR TRANSLATION	EXAMPLE SENTENCE	NOTES

Photocopiable

Remember to use the Notes column

Use the A–Z Data system to write down the words and expressions that are important for you.

	WORD/EXPRESSION PRONUNCIATION
	PART OF SPEECH
	PICTURE, MEANING OR TRANSLATION
	EXAMPLE SENTENCE
	NOTES

In the A–Z Data system you can create your own personal dictionary.

- **Look at the example in the chart and read the information.**

Check the spelling.
Write in the word stress and pronunciation when it is useful.

Draw a picture, write the meaning in English or a translation.

WORD/ EXPRESSION PRONUNCIATION	PART OF SPEECH	PICTURE, MEANING OR TRANSLATION	EXAMPLE SENTENCE	NOTES
worry /ʌ/	v.	(picture of worried face)	Don't _worry_ about your exams. It'll be OK.	to worry _about_ = to be worried about Don't worry about your exam. (spoken)

Is it a noun (n.), a verb (v.), a phrasal verb, an adjective (adj.) or an adverb (adv.), etc.?

Use the word /expression in sentences about your life and interests.
When you find a new word / expression in a sentence you read or hear, write down the whole sentence.

Write notes about the word / expression, e.g. opposites, grammar points, spoken/written language.

- **Look at the following:**

    weak   to turn on

    Where would you write them in the A–Z?
    What information is important to write about them?

- **Find them in the A–Z and check your ideas.**

- **Put the following word and expression, and information about them in the A–Z Data system.**

    stomach-ache   to have a row

- **Check your answers in the key at the end of Dictionary skills.**

Use your dictionary to check spelling and pronunciation

7 You can write words with their opposites.
   ▶ See **A–Z, Topic pages**.

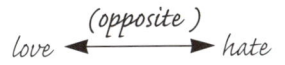

   love ◀— *(opposite)* —▶ hate

8 You can use pictures and diagrams.
   ▶ See **A–Z, Word web, Topic pages**.

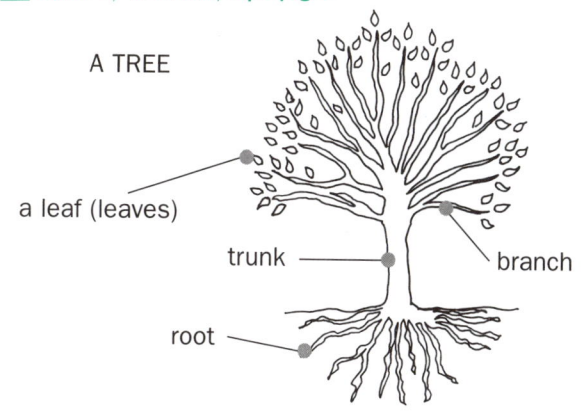

   A TREE

   a leaf (leaves)
   trunk
   branch
   root

9 You can write lists of words with their translations.

   cloudy = nuvoloso
   mirror = かがみ
   shout = crier

10 You can write a definition in English.
   ▶ See **A–Z, Power verbs, Phrasal verbs**.

   to repeat = to do again

11 You can write the different parts of speech, for example, noun (n.), adjective (adj.), verb (v.).
   ▶ See **A–Z, Word-builder**.

   translate (v.) translation (n.) translator (n. person)

12 You can write words with their partners.
   ▶ See **A–Z, Topic pages, Power verbs, Word partners**.

   go to
   make a mistake
   a high mountain

VOCABULARY STRATEGIES

- Look at the following vocabulary strategies.
- Which ones do you use? Why?
- Which new ones will you try? Why?
- Find examples of the strategies in the Vocabulary section to see how to use them.

1. You can make a sentence with the new word or expression.
   ▶ See **A–Z, Power verbs, Phrasal verbs**.
   I put the letter in an <u>envelope</u> and then I posted it.

2. You can make notes about how to use the new word or expression.
   ▶ See **A–Z, Topic pages**.
   information NOT ~~informations~~ (always uncountable)

3. You can mark the stress.
   ▶ See **A–Z, Word-builder, Dictionary skills, Stress patterns**.
   photógraphy

4. You can write the pronunciation.
   ▶ See **Topic pages, Dictionary skills, Pronunciation table**.
   photography
   /fəˈtɒgrəfi/

5. You can organise new vocabulary in topic groups.
   ▶ See **Word web, Topic pages**.

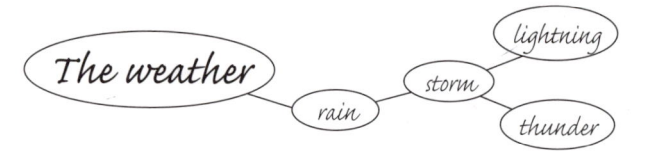

   The weather — rain — storm — lightning / thunder

6. You can write words with similar meanings.
   ▶ See **Word web, Topic pages**.
   large = big

Select the strategies which are right for you

wordflo™

YOUR PERSONAL ENGLISH ORGANISER

TEACHER'S GUIDE

STEVE SMITH AND JACQUELINE SMITH

with additional material by
GAIL ELLIS and BARBARA SINCLAIR
RICHARD ACKLAM

LONGMAN

Addison Wesley Longman Limited
Edinburgh Gate
Harlow
Essex CM20 2JE
England
and Associated Companies throughout the World.

© Addison Wesley Longman Limited 1997
All rights reserved; no part of this publication may be reproduced, stored in a retrieval system, or transmitted in any form or by any means, electronic, mechanical, photocopying, recording, or otherwise without the prior written permission of the Publisher.

First published 1998
Second impression 1998
Wordflo is a trademark of Addison Wesley Longman Limited

Photocopying
The Publishers grant permission for the photocopying of those pages marked 'photocopiable' according to the following conditions. Individual purchasers may make copies for their own use or for use by classes they teach, but this permission does not extend to additional schools or branches.

Under no circumstances may any part of this book be photocopied for resale.

Set in Franklin Gothic, Caflisch
Printed in Spain by Mateu Cromo

ISBN 0582 32887X

Designed by Shireen Nathoo Design

Acknowledgements
We are indebted to Cambridge University Press for permission to reproduce adapted extracts from *Games for Language Learning* by A Wright, D Betterbridge and M Buckley (1996) and *Grammar Games* by Mario Rinvolucri (1996).

INTRODUCTION

WHAT IS *WORDFLO*?

Wordflo is a personal English language organiser. It promotes learner independence and aids learner development through the use of **Data systems**.

These **Data systems** provide user-friendly formats for learners to record, categorise and analyse the new language they encounter in their courses, their reading and their travels.

WHAT *WORDFLO* CONTAINS

The main sections, which are marked by tabs for easy access, are:

Personal (for personal data)
Notes (for quickly writing down information which can then be transferred to the **Data systems**)
Learning techniques (learner training strategies)
Vocabulary (concentrates not only on single words, but also on 'chunks' of language, including phrasal verbs, high frequency generative verbs and collocations. There is also a **Dictionary skills** section which includes a **Pronunciation chart**, a **homophone chart** and a **Stress patterns Data system**)
Useful phrases (a personalised phrasebook and functions bank)
Grammar (a handy, interactive reference to the major grammar problems at intermediate level)
Self-correction (for recording selected errors and corrections)

The **Vocabulary** and **Grammar** sections contain several easily retrievable sub-sections, offering learners with different learning styles a variety of options for recording language.

KEY CONCEPTS BEHIND *WORDFLO*

- **Learner independence**

Wordflo prepares and encourages students to go on learning outside the classroom and after the course is over by providing them with strategies. It helps to develop their confidence and decision-making skills because they decide what to record, and where to record it. It trains them to learn more efficiently by giving them an *active role* in the learning process.

- **Organising language**
Research in cognitive psychology shows that writing down and organising new information helps students to remember. *Wordflo* provides students with many different ways of organising language and encourages them to identify those which are most effective for their particular learning styles.

- **Personal involvement**
Learners can more easily recall language if it is learnt in contexts which have some personal significance. *Wordflo* encourages learners to choose items that are important to them, and when recording these items in the **Data systems**, to try to relate them to their lives.

- **Vocabulary**
Wordflo recognises the importance of vocabulary in language learning. It focuses on the necessity to learn not just individual words, but also 'chunks' of language. The **Data systems** – especially those in **Word combinations** – give students the opportunity to work with these chunks.
Wordflo encourages learners to focus on high frequency language such as **Power verbs** (e.g. put, get) which form the basis of many chunks of language.

- **Grammar**
Wordflo also recognises the importance of grammar in language learning, and the **Grammar section** provides both a reference guide and the opportunity for students to record personalised examples of key structures.

- **The teacher's role**
It is essential for teachers to spend some time on introducing *Wordflo* to their students. Students should be encouraged to try out the different systems. Experimenting with the systems is an important way for students to acquire new learning strategies. Teachers should also carefully monitor their students' use of *Wordflo* over time, to check that students are benefiting from it fully.

- **Growing with *Wordflo***
The **Data systems** in *Wordflo* are not exercises to be completed in one lesson, or one week, or even one month. As with a traditional notebook, learners store items as they encounter them. One advantage of this process is that learners must return again and again to the pages, looking at items they previously recorded and seeing how they relate to newer items. *Wordflo* grows as the learner's knowledge of the language increases.

- **Monitoring learners' work**
Wordflo is the learner's place to think, experiment, and organise. What students write in *Wordflo* does not have to be perfect to be useful. If, for example, a learner misspells a word when writing an example sentence for a new vocabulary item in the **A–Z Data system**, the example sentence is still valuable as it should help the student learn the meaning of the new item. As the learner progresses in English, she/he might even notice the misspelled word and be able to correct it. From time to time, you may want to take in your students' *Wordflo* (or the relevant detachable pages – remember to get them to write their names at the top). We suggest that you take in *Wordflo* or *Wordflo* pages to prepare for some of the games and activities and **Self-correction** suggestions in this Teacher's Guide.

INTRODUCING WORDFLO

You can introduce *Wordflo* to your students at any time, but the best time to do so is at the beginning of a course, so that students have the whole course to learn how to organise their learning.

INTRODUCTORY LESSON 1
Introducing *Wordflo* through student notebooks

Time: steps 1–4 approximately 20 minutes;
       step 5 approximately 10–15 minutes.

1. Ask some volunteers to pass around their notebooks.
2. Students comment on similarities and differences.

3. Start a discussion on student notebooks (possibly in L1). The following questions can help you get started:
   Why do you write things down during your English lessons?
   What kinds of things do you write down?
   Do you often go back and look at what you've written down?
   If so, do you often make changes to that information (adding or correcting, for example)?
   Is it easy for you to find what you want in your notebook? Why or why not?
   Is it important to have an organised notebook? If so, why?
   How do you organise information in your notebook?
   How could you improve your organisation?
   If you could plan the ideal language learning notebook, what would it be like?

4. During the discussion, write on the board the ideas that students come up with about improving their organisation.

5. Give out or go through *Wordflo*. In small groups, students look through their notebooks and decide where and how they could record some of that information in *Wordflo*. Point out that they don't have to transfer all of the information from their notebooks to *Wordflo* (unless they really want to!). From now on they can record all new language directly in their *Wordflo*. Explain that they can write down new language on the **Notes** pages and later transfer it to the **Data systems**.

INTRODUCTORY LESSON 2
Designing Wordflo

Time: approximately 25–30 minutes

1. Divide the class into pairs or small groups.

2. Give each pair/group two sets of cards, one with the names of some of the *Wordflo* sections on them, and the other with the names of some of the *Wordflo* sub-sections and features, before they have seen *Wordflo*.
   Section cards: **Personal, Notes, Learning techniques, Vocabulary, Useful phrases, Grammar, Self-correction.**
   Sub-sections and features cards: **A place to write your name and address, a place to note things down quickly, a place**

to learn about learning, a place to write words for shopping, a place to write corrections, **A–Z, Topics, Word-building, Word combinations, Present simple/continuous, Conditionals, Countable/Uncountable nouns, Comparatives/Superlatives, Modal verbs, Irregular verb list**.

3. Have a whole-class discussion about what the names mean and refer to.
4. The pairs/groups place the sub-section/feature cards with the section cards they think they relate to. This will have the following benefits: it will make them categorise – a technique they will use again and again in *Wordflo*, it will give them an understanding of the organisational principles of *Wordflo*, before they have even seen it.
5. A few pairs/groups tell the class which cards they matched and why.
6. Hand out *Wordflo* to all the students. Encourage them to explore *Wordflo*. Ask them how the structure of *Wordflo* is similar to or different from the structures they created with their cards. Ask a few pairs/groups for the reasons for their decisions.

INTRODUCTORY LESSON 3
Stage 1: Introducing *Wordflo* through a personal organiser and quiz.

Time: approximately 20 minutes

1. Ask students what a 'personal organiser' is and how it works. (Show an actual example if possible.)
2. Elicit as much information as possible from students. Make sure you establish that:
   a) it helps you organise things.
   b) it can hold information about different things.
   c) you can add notes/information to it.
   d) it's a good idea to keep it with you most of the time.
3. Ask students to imagine that if there was one for English language learners, what it might contain.
4. Write up ideas on the board.

5. Give out copies of *Wordflo*. Students look through it and see how it compares to their ideas.

6. Establish that *Wordflo* is organised like this:

> PERSONAL
> NOTES
> LEARNING TECHNIQUES
> VOCABULARY   A–Z
>   Topics
>   Word-building
>   Word combinations
>   Dictionary skills
> USEFUL PHRASES
> GRAMMAR
> SELF-CORRECTION

Stage 2: Establishing the contents of *Wordflo*.
Time: approximately 40 minutes

1. Get students to do the quiz at the end of this introduction either a) in pairs in class or b) for homework.
   Answers
   1. Personal
   2. Notes
   3. Learning techniques
   4. Learning techniques
   5. Learning techniques
   6. Vocabulary section
   7. Vocabulary – Word web
   8. Word combinations – Phrasal verbs
   9. Dictionary skills – Pronunciation chart
   10. Dictionary skills
   11. Useful phrases
   12. Grammar section
   13. Grammar – Irregular verbs

2. Get feedback from the class.

PLANNING WHEN AND HOW TO USE *WORDFLO*
Time: approximately 20 minutes

Discuss with students what they (and you) think they should 'do' with *Wordflo* over the coming week or so. Write all the ideas on the board. Then sort them out into a concrete 'plan'. (You may wish to encourage students to use the *Wordflo* Weekly planner).

QUIZ

1. Where do you write your name and address?
2. Where can you quickly write down interesting new words that you want to remember?
3. Where can you find out what kind of language learner you are?
4. Where can you work out how much time you have to use *Wordflo*?
5. Where can you see an example of a student's *Wordflo* learning plan?
6. Where can you see examples of many different ways of writing down new vocabulary?
7. Where can you see an example of a Word web about 'time'?
8. Where can you find information about/examples of phrasal verbs?
9. Where can you find out how to pronounce the different sounds of English?
10. Where do you find out what a dictionary can tell you?
11. Where do you find out some useful expressions/questions to use in the classroom?
12. Where can you find information about the Past simple and Past continuous?
13 Where can you find a list of irregular Past simple and past participle forms?

Photocopiable

LEARNING TECHNIQUES

The **Learning techniques** section provides students with a general learning strategy, which they can apply to their English language learning and the contents of *Wordflo*.

The goals of **learner training** are to help learners become better and more independent in their language learning. In keeping with these goals, this section involves students in a process of reflection on and experimentation with vocabulary and grammar learning strategies of their choice. This can help them become more aware of how they like to learn, their learning needs, and the strategies which work best for them.

LANGUAGE LEARNING STRATEGIES

There are many different learning strategies and several attempts have been made to classify these. Generally speaking, however, there are two major categories of learning strategies which are most relevant for students working with *Wordflo*: metacognitive and cognitive strategies.

- **Metacognitive strategies**
These are the strategies which involve learners in thinking about their learning: for example, what are the factors which affect their learning? What are their needs? How can they plan their learning? How can they evaluate their learning and monitor their progress? What do they need to do next?

- **Cognitive strategies**
These are the strategies which involve learners in actually *doing* things with the language in order to learn it, such as doing a **Word web**, writing vocabulary lists, doing grammar exercises.

- **Strategies in *Wordflo***
The activities in *Wordflo* provide development in both metacognitive and cognitive strategies. Many language teaching materials tend to focus on the development of cognitive strategies only so that students never have the opportunity to think about what they are doing in the classroom and why. Research has shown that courses which combine the

development of cognitive strategies with metacognitive strategies help students to manage their own learning more successfully. Students gradually discover more about themselves as learners, about how to learn a language and can take on more responsibility for their own learning.

In order to help students in this way, they need to be *consciously* aware of what they are doing when they learn. This requires an *explicit* approach to learner training. An explicit approach to learner training is one where the students are informed of the purpose and usefulness of a particular strategy, so that they are able to transfer it to other language learning tasks independently.

In order to highlight the social nature of language learning some optional language practice activities have been suggested which involve students in communication tasks with each other and their teacher.

YOUR GUIDE TO SUCCESSFUL LANGUAGE LEARNING

These tips list a variety of characteristics which research has shown successful language learners have, as well as learning strategies they use. In particular, the list highlights important metacognitive strategies. These are exemplified throughout the **Learning techniques** section of *Wordflo*.

- **Aims**
- to help students to become aware of ways in which they can help themselves develop more effective learning habits.
- to introduce or revise key vocabulary related to language learning:
  e.g.: *to be realistic, resources, to practise, to take a risk, to make a mistake, to worry about something, to review something.*

  to prepare students for the **How do you like to learn? Quiz**.

- **Suggestions for use**
1. Discussion: ask students to brainstorm what they think a successful language learner is and does. Allow the students

to use their mother tongue, if necessary, so that they can express their ideas in a meaningful way.

2. Elicit ideas, put these ideas on the board and check vocabulary. Suggest some examples to start with:
   A successful learner is someone who:
   – *learns something every day*
   – *keeps a vocabulary book*
   etc.

   Suggest students can use the ideas in **Your Guide to successful language learning** to help them.

3. Ask students to look at the **Guide**:
   Ask them how they feel about the list of tips:
   – *which ones do you do already?*
   – *do any of them surprise you? Why?*
   – *which ones do you think are most important for you personally?*
   – *are there any other tips you would like to add to the list?*

- **Optional Language Practice**

Ask students to work in pairs and ask each other questions based on the tips in the **Guide**. This will involve them in transforming imperative statements in the Present simple to questions:
e.g.: *What do you like doing....? Are you realistic...?*

QUIZ

This **Quiz** incorporates information on aspects of four broad learning styles with feedback in the form of practical suggestions.

- **Aims**
– to help students know more about themselves as learners and to discover the strategies which suit them best.

- **Suggestions for use**
1. Ask students to look at questions a) to f) in the **Quiz** and decide which best describe them.

2. Ask them to say why they have chosen their answers. Use questions like:
   - *How do you know you like to learn in this way?*
   - *Can you give us an example of the type of thing you do?*

   It is important to ask these questions to encourage the students to think about their learning habits. Discussing the questions in class can help students find out more about themselves and their classmates as learners. It also enables them to find out more about different ways of learning. Again, allow the students to use their mother tongue, if appropriate, so they can express their ideas well.

3. Ask them to read the corresponding advice on the next page.
4. Ask them to form small groups according to their learning style to discuss in more detail what they have found out and think about other ways they can help themselves.
5. Ask the groups to share their ideas with the rest of the class.

WHAT CAN YOU DO TO LEARN ENGLISH?

This provides students with an overview of the **Plan – Do – Review** cycle in learning. This general strategy for learning is important because it can be used as a framework for learning *any* subject, including language learning.

Ask students to look at this information and check that they understand it.

PLAN

Planning is a metacognitive strategy which is crucial to successful learning. However, developing this in students is very often neglected – traditionally, planning learning is seen as the teacher's responsibility. There is a need to involve the students actively in the planning of their own learning, so that they become more aware of the factors affecting their learning, such as their personal needs, wants, time, learning styles and resources. In this way, they will learn to become more independent.

WHAT DO YOU NEED TO DO?

1. Ask students to read the text and look at the diagram on the importance of developing vocabulary and grammar.
2. Ask students to think about their general English language needs and tick the appropriate box(es).
3. Ask students to list specific topics and situations they need to develop vocabulary for. Some examples have been provided.
4. Ask students to list areas of grammar they want to improve. Some examples have been provided.

PLAN YOUR LEARNING TIME

1. Make sure that students understand how important it is to be realistic about how much time they have for learning English.
2. Ask students to calculate their *Wordflo* time by completing the chart.

- **Optional Language Practice**

Ask students to work in pairs to ask and answer the questions in the chart. For example: *How many hours do you spend sleeping in a typical week? And washing and dressing?*

Students might like to collect the information from their partner and collate it into a class survey or chart which could be displayed in the classroom. This could then be interpreted by students by asking *How many students spend 60 hours sleeping?* and so on.

WHAT RESOURCES DO YOU NEED?

1. Ask students to discuss the different resources they use and need to learn English. Introduce or revise vocabulary such as *dictionary, bilingual, monolingual, grammar book, video, radio, magazines, newspapers, books, native speakers,*

English club, etc.

2. Ask students to look at and answer the questions.
3. You might like to show the students examples of good reference materials and other resources.

SELECT YOUR STRATEGY

1. Make sure students understand what is meant by a vocabulary strategy and a grammar strategy:
   A vocabulary strategy is what a learner does in order to learn new vocabulary, e.g. write a list with translations.
   A grammar strategy is what a learner does to learn grammar structures, e.g.: do a grammar exercise from a book.
2. Ask students to discuss how they learn new words and grammar structures.
3. Ask students to look at the **Vocabulary** and **Grammar** sections of *Wordflo* for examples of strategies that they can try.

PLAN YOUR REVIEW TIME

1. Ask students if and when they review their work.
2. Ask them to look at the graph and ask the following questions:
   - *How many review times are suggested?*
   - *When is the ideal time for the first review?*
   - *When is the second review? etc.*
   - *How are you going to plan review sessions into your WORDFLO time?*

DO

This section involves students in doing a plan for a learning activity of their own choice. A learner training activity (Françoise's plan) provides them with an example of how this can be done. Completing the plan is a metacognitive strategy which prepares the students and leads them into experimenting with the cognitive strategies of their choice.

1. Ask students to read about Françoise and to discuss the topics and situations where she needs English on her study trip.
2. Ask students to look at the plan, referring them back to the **What can you do to learn English?** page.
3. Highlight the importance of the review times referring them back to the **Plan your review time** graph.
4. Ask students to look at Françoise's **Word web**. Refer them to the **Word web Data system**, if necessary.
5. Ask students to decide what they want to learn and then do their plan for the strategy they have selected for learning it, using the blank chart provided. Advise as necessary.

It would be unrealistic to expect students to do a plan in this detail for every activity, but the aim here is to model a useful strategy which they can use as a basis for future planning.

REVIEW

This section demonstrates the metacognitive strategy of reviewing. Regular reviewing is crucial to successful learning. However, students are rarely encouraged to consider the benefits of reviewing systematically or to consider when the most effective time to do this is.

1. Ask students to read Françoise's comments. This provides a model for the kind of reflection that is important.
2. Ask students to work in pairs and ask each other the four review questions about their own strategy.
3. Ask students to look at how Françoise has transferred her reflections to her review chart.
4. Ask students to complete their own review chart, using the blank one provided.

It would be unrealistic to expect students to complete a review chart in this detail for every activity, but again, the aim here is to model a useful strategy which they can use as a basis for future reviewing.

MAKING PROGRESS

This page demonstrates the on-going cyclical nature of the **Plan – Do – Review** general learning strategy, and how this enables students to break down their learning into manageable chunks, and to see their progress. This, in turn, enhances students' motivation to continue learning.

- Explain to the students how important it is to use the **Plan – Do – Review** cycle regularly.
- Remind them that they should carry on using their *Wordflo* and adding new things to it.

A–Z

In the **A–Z Data system** learners create their own personalised dictionary.

- **Aims**
  - to enable students to record new vocabulary in an organised and easily retrievable format.
  - to encourage students to record meanings in several ways, rather than always relying on L1 translation.
  - to encourage students to write an example sentence (using the item in context will help students to remember it).
  - to encourage students to record important features of vocabulary (part of speech, pronunciation, synonyms, relevant grammatical information, etc.).

- **Suggestions for use**

Go through the introductory page of the **A–Z Data system** with your students before trying the suggestion below.

1. Pre-teach key vocabulary items from a reading or listening text or a discussion topic, eliciting from the learners wherever possible.

2. From these new items, help the class choose between six and ten useful items that they want to learn. Learners record these in the first column of **A–Z**.

3. After working on the reading/listening/speaking activity, ask learners in pairs or small groups to fill in the other columns of the chart. They can use their dictionaries once they have filled in as much as they can from memory. In the case of reading, they can also go back to the text to see the words/expressions in context and copy the sentence they appear in, to reinforce that context.

4. Get feedback from the class. You may want to give students further information for the Notes column to ensure relevant grammatical information, collocations, synonyms and opposites, etc. have been covered.

- **Homework**
1. For a reading assignment, tell students to record in the **A–Z** between six and ten new vocabulary items from the reading. They should fill in all the columns. Students record only the words they think are important to learn.
2. In class the next day, ask students which vocabulary items they have recorded and why.

This activity will encourage students to use the **A–Z** on their own and to decide which vocabulary is important for them.

GAMES/ACTIVITIES
Learner-centred Quiz
Time: Preparation 30 minutes to 1 hour; in class 15–20 minutes

You can easily prepare learner-centred quizzes on vocabulary items that all students have recorded in their **A–Z Data system.**

1. Students hand in their best example sentences from the work of the last week, month, etc. This has the benefit of making them go back and review their work.
2. From these, choose the best example sentences for the words that you wish to focus on. Use these to prepare your quiz, correcting any mistakes and leaving a gap for the vocabulary items.
3. Photocopy and give out the quiz.

The quiz exposes students to both sentences they have written and to those of other students in the class. Students also receive gentle correction of any errors through seeing the correct version of their work.

Example
To revise the word 'snore'.
Student sentence: *Some people snore when they are sleep on their backs.*
Quiz sentence: *Some people _____ when they sleep on their backs.* (Hint: they make a noise.)

TOPICS

WORD WEBS/TOPIC PAGES

A **Word web** is a visual representation of the relationship between words and expressions in a particular lexical field. **Topic pages** serve the same purpose, and give learners the chance to use a variety of techniques for recording words – pictures, symbols, mini-word webs, etc.

- **Aims**
  - to help students remember new vocabulary by encouraging them to organise it in a visually interesting way.
  - to encourage learners to think about the relationships between vocabulary items in a lexical field.

- **Suggestions for use**

Go through the introductory pages with your students before trying the suggestions below. These suggestions can be followed for either **Word webs** or **Topic pages**.

Suggestion 1

Time: 15–25 minutes, steps 1–3; 10–15 minutes, steps 4–5

1. Before a reading or listening task, write the topic on the board.

2. Students generate a list of words and expressions connected to the topic, either calling out items as a whole class, or working first in pairs before suggesting items to put on the board. If students want to know a particular word in English, tell them.

3. Each student creates a **Word web/Topic page** with the words/expressions on the board.

4. During the first reading or listening, students check which items in their **Word webs/Topic pages** appear in the text and note down any other words/expressions connected to the topic that the class did not come up with.

5. They add the new words/expressions to their **Word webs/Topic pages** and then compare their work with that of other students.

6. Remind students that they can add other items later on, as they learn more words and expressions related to the topic.

Suggestion 2

Time: 15–25 minutes

1. Suggest a topic you have recently worked on with your students and let them create their own **Word webs/Topic pages**.

2. Students walk around and look at each others' work. Encourage questions about vocabulary items that they don't know or don't remember, or about the reasons for the connection between words.

3. Students sit down and add items they have learned from their classmates to their **Word webs/Topic pages**.

4. Remind students that they can add other items later on, as they learn more words and expressions related to the topic.

- **Homework**

1. Students create **Word webs/Topic pages** for a vocabulary area they have recently studied.

2. In the next lesson, students look at each others' **Word webs/Topic pages** and vote on the best one. In this way, they learn from each other by seeing which words and expressions other students included and how they connected them. In addition, this period of comparing each others' work gives you time to check it.

GAMES/ACTIVITIES

Categories

Time: 5–20 minutes

1. The whole class thinks of some categories (suggest some yourself to start them off, e.g. food, countries, animals, verbs, adjectives, etc.).

2. Divide the class into two or three teams.

3. Choose a letter of the alphabet, tell the students the letter, and say "GO!".
4. The teams have to write one word in each category beginning with that letter.
5. The first team to finish shout "STOP!", and the other teams have to stop.
6. Check the words of the first team to finish. Award one point for each correct word which only that team have got. Don't award points for words which other teams have also got.
7. Start again with a new letter.
8. Students record new vocabulary in the **Topic pages** and/or **Word webs**.

See also **Vocabulary Battle** in **Vocabulary Games**.

WORD-BUILDING

Encourage your students to look carefully at **Prefixes** and **Suffixes** before using the **Word-builder**. If your students need further practice in identifying suffixes or parts of speech, write up the following list of words. Students underline the suffixes. Then they write *noun*, *adjective*, *verb* or *adverb* next to each of the words. Check their work.

1. categorise
2. freedom
3. imagination
4. beautiful
5. slowly
6. writer
7. Mexican
8. happiness
9. financial
10. talkative

Answers

1.	-ise	verb	6.	-er	writer
2.	-dom	noun	7.	-an	noun or adjective
3.	-ation	noun	8.	-ness	noun
4.	-ful	adjective	9.	-ial	adjective
5.	-ly	adverb	10.	-ative	adjective

WORD-BUILDER

The **Word-builder** is a table in which learners record words that can be formed from a root word. Go through the introductory page with your students before trying the suggestions below.

- **Aims**
- to expand learners' vocabulary by getting the most out of words they already know
- to train learners to understand parts of speech
- to train learners to use prefixes and suffixes
- to train learners to anticipate word formation patterns

- **Suggestions for use**

Time: 10–15 minutes

1. Choose six to ten words which learners have recently studied. These words should generate other useful words by changing the part of speech and/or adding suffixes and prefixes.

2. Draw the **Word-builder** on the board.
3. Give students the first word and ask them what part of speech it is. Write it in the appropriate column.
4. Ask students what the corresponding noun/verb/adjective etc. is. Encourage them to guess how to make the verb a noun, or the noun an adjective, etc., basing their guesses on the **Suffixes** chart and on other words they know.
5. Write the words in the appropriate columns. In some cases, some columns may not have any words.
6. If it is appropriate, elicit words formed by adding prefixes.
7. Point out that some words from the same root change their meanings when they change the part of speech (for example, *book* [n] and to *book* [v]). Make sure you discuss differences of meaning with your students.
8. Follow this procedure for each of your chosen words. Learners write all the words in their **Word-builders**. Where there are stress shifts or difficult sounds, make sure your students note down the pronunciation.
9. (Optional) In class, or for homework, students record in the **A–Z** any of the words described in step 7.

- **Homework**
1. From the work you did in class, choose one or two useful word formation patterns (for example, many nouns ending in *-ance* or *-ence* can be made into adjectives by changing the ending to *-ant* or *-ent*).
2. Ask students to think of six to ten other words that follow the same patterns and write them in the **Word-builder**.
3. Students report back in class the next day and write new words they learn from each other in the **Word-builder**.

GAMES/ACTIVITIES

The Word-building game

Time: 15–20 minutes

1. Divide the class into groups of three or four.
2. Give each group eight words to write in their **Word-builder** (some verbs, some adjectives, some adverbs, etc.) from a vocabulary area, listening or reading text they have recently worked on.
3. Give them twelve minutes to build as many words as they can from the eight words given.
4. Give each group a good learners' dictionary such as *Longman Active Study Dictionary* to check their ideas.
5. The groups get a point for every correct word they have written. The group with the most points wins.

Prefix dominoes

Time: 25–35 minutes

1. Prepare a set of "dominoes" on cards for each group of five to six students. Each domino should have one adjective and one prefix (See the list opposite). They do not necessarily have to form a word. For example:

popular	ir
legal	un

2. Include a few extra dominoes with only prefixes on them. Example

un	im

3. Photocopy **How to play Prefix dominoes** (at the end of this section). Give a copy to each student and a set of dominoes to each group of five or six. Go through this with them to ensure they understand the instructions.
4. While students play, check the words that they form. If you

find an incorrect combination, the students must take back all the dominoes laid from that point on and start again from there.

5. If the game gets blocked before any student has put down all their dominoes, the person who has the fewest dominoes wins, and they start a new game.

6. After most of the groups have finished, stop the game and tell the students in each group to pronounce and define each of the words formed.

7. Students write new words or words they had difficulty remembering during the game in their **Word-builders**. They then build other words from these where possible. Students can also record words in **A–Z**.

You can choose some of the words and prefixes in this list to prepare your cards. Choose words that your students already know, plus a few new ones that you wish to introduce:

il...legal	il...legible	il...literate	il...logical
im...moral	im...mortal	im...possible	im...patient
im...polite	in...accurate	in...appropriate	in...capable
in...compatible	in...complete	in...considerate	in...convenient
in...correct	in...decisive	in...definite	in...dependent
in...direct	in...effective	in...efficient	in...expensive
in...secure	in...sensitive	in...sincere	in...tolerant
in...visible	ir...rational	ir...relevant	ir...responsible
un...able	un...acceptable	un...believable	un...comfortable
un...employed	un...fair	un...fortunate	un...happy
un...healthy	un...lucky	un...necessary	un...pleasant
un...popular	un...predictable	un...reasonable	un...reliable

HOW TO PLAY PREFIX DOMINOES

Student 1

1. Shuffle the dominoes and give four to each player.
2. Place one domino on the table, face up so that the word shows. Put the remaining dominoes in a pile, face down so the words do not show.

Student 2

1. Try to put one of your dominoes next to the one on the table, to form a word.
   Example:

legal	un	popular	ir

   These two dominoes form the word *unpopular*. If you can put down a domino, the next player goes.
2. If you cannot put down a domino, pick another one from the pile. You may put this one down if you can form a correct word. If not, you must keep it and try to put it down on another turn.
3. The next player goes.

All the players continue in this way. The first player to put down all of his/her dominoes wins.

WORD COMBINATIONS

Word combinations consists of three **Data systems** for recording different types of frequent and useful collocations:

Phrasal verbs
Power verbs (very common verbs e.g. have, make, do, get, put, take etc.) that often combine with other words to make expressions and idioms);
Word partners (common collocations – adjective/noun, verb/adjective, adverb/adjective, adverb/adjective/noun, noun/noun, etc.).

- **Aims**
- to train learners to think in terms of chunks of language rather than discrete vocabulary items.
- to provide learners with a format for recording collocations.

- **Suggestions for Use**

Go through the introductory activities for each of the **Data systems** before trying the suggestions below.

PHRASAL VERBS

Time: 20–30 minutes

1. Prepare a list of four to five phrasal verbs connected to your classwork.
2. Write them mixed-up on the board.
   Example   bring   on
             about   carry
             get   turn
             take   over
             up   away
3. Divide the class into groups of three.
4. Give each group a dictionary (learners' dictionaries are best for this activity). [▶ **Dictionary skills**.]
5. The groups find as many possible partnerships as they can among the words on the board, while you monitor and give feedback. They will find many phrasal verbs other than those on your list.

6. Learners record the most useful new phrasal verbs in the **Phrasal verbs Data system**.

POWER VERBS
Time: 20–30 minutes

1. Prepare a list of expressions/idioms made from the power verbs in this section that you wish to introduce or review.
2. Write them mixed-up on the board.

Example	give	get
	off	have
	instructions	do
	time	well
	put	tired

3. Repeat steps 3–6, above.

WORD PARTNERS
Time: 20–30 minutes

1. Prepare a list of word partners that you wish to introduce or review.
2. Write them on the board in a mixed-up fashion.

Example	be in	life
	night	spare
	club	and day
	time	table

3. Repeat steps 3–6, above.

- **Homework**
1. **In class** students look at the **Phrasal verb** and/or **Power verb Data systems** where they have recently recorded items you have worked on.
2. Elicit phrasal verbs and power verbs.
3. On the board, show students some questions they could ask each other, using the phrasal verbs/power verbs which would

produce some interesting answers.
Example
- Did you <u>have a good time</u> last weekend? Why or why not?
- Do you <u>put off</u> certain things? Which things? Why?
- What time do you <u>get up</u> at the weekend?

4. Tell a few students to ask these questions around the class. They should ask a few different people the same question, so that everyone can hear the different answers they produce.

5. **For homework**, students write interesting questions with other phrasal verbs/power verbs from their **Data systems**.

6. In the next lesson, call on different students to ask their questions around the class.

GAMES/ACTIVITIES

The Word combinations memory game

Time: steps 1–3, 15–20 minutes; steps 4–6, 10 minutes.

N.B. The instructions below describe how the game can be used to work on **Phrasal verbs**, but the same procedure can be used to work on **Power verbs** or **Word partners** with a change of cards.

1. Before the lesson in which you play this game, monitor the **Phrasal verbs Data system** in your students' *Wordflo* to see which phrasal verbs they have been recording.

2. Based on your findings, prepare a set of cards for each group. Use two different coloured cards. Write phrasal verbs on one and definitions of the phrasal verbs on the other colour of card. You will need about ten phrasal verbs with their definitions for each set.

3. Divide the class into groups of three or four and give each group a set of cards.

4. Give each group a copy of **How to play the Word combinations memory game**. Ensure students understand the instructions.

5. Students play the game.

6. (Optional) At the end of the game, the whole class can look at the phrasal verb cards, with or without the definition cards, and, working in pairs or small groups, students create **Mind stories** [▶ **Vocabulary games**.] using as many of the phrasal verbs as possible. The pairs/small groups can then tell their stories to the class and write them up for homework.

HOW TO PLAY THE
WORD COMBINATIONS MEMORY GAME

Student 1

Shuffle the cards and lay them out on a desk. Put them face down so you cannot see the words.

Student 2

Turn over two cards. If they make a word combination, pick them up. You get one point for each of the two cards. For an extra point, you must make a sentence using the word combination.

1. If the two cards you turn over do not make a word combination, turn them face down again *without changing their position on the desk.*
2. The next player goes.
3. The game continues until there are no more cards. The winner is the player with the most points.
4. You can then record the word combinations and the bonus sentences in one or more of the **Word combinations Data systems** in your *Wordflo*.

Photocopiable

DICTIONARY SKILLS

THE ROLE OF DICTIONARIES IN THE EFL CLASSROOM

The student's dictionary can be a key element in helping the learner to become independent. There are now a wide range of dictionaries available for different ages and different levels.

The more that dictionaries can be incorporated as a regular part of classroom work, the more students will become familiar and comfortable with using dictionaries.

Wordflo contains a short dictionary section aimed at acquainting students with some of the important features that good dictionaries have to offer. This, however, is just a beginning and should be followed up by teachers as appropriate in their individual classes.

IDEAS FOR USING *WORDFLO* DICTIONARY SKILLS SECTION IN CLASS

Ask students what different information a good dictionary will contain. Put their ideas on the board.

Then get students to look through the **Dictionary tips** section and the following dictionary extracts. Tell them to find all the extra information that this dictionary gives which they didn't think of. Get open-class feedback.

An alternative way of getting students to look at the **What your dictionary tells you** pages would be to photocopy the pages and cut off the third column. This could be cut up into individual sections and students then work together in pairs to match these sections to the appropriately highlighted dictionary extract.

Ask students what dictionaries they have or have used in the past. Get feedback about what they think of them, how useful they are, what information they give etc.

If appropriate, recommend a suitable dictionary. The dictionary entries in *Wordflo* all come from the *Longman Active Study Dictionary*.

Take in a set of dictionaries if possible. Students use these dictionaries or their own to attempt the **Something to try** section. You could organise students into teams to do this, where they try to complete all the tasks as quickly as possible.

GENERAL DICTIONARY SKILLS DEVELOPMENT

Encourage students to use dictionaries in class whenever possible/appropriate. For example, when introducing a new set of vocabulary, give different words to small groups of students for them to find out the meaning, part of speech, pronunciation etc. They can then get into new groups and 'teach' one another the new items. Remind students to keep a record of all the new words they learn in the appropriate section of *Wordflo*.

When dealing with reading texts it is important to encourage students to be able to deduce the meaning of unknown words from the surrounding context e.g. *The food was so bland that he had to put lots of salt on it*. In cases like this it may be appropriate to ask students to suggest possible meanings of the target word based on the context and then get them to look in their dictionaries to check their ideas.

When marking students' written work you may like to highlight parts where students have made mistakes with spelling, the meaning of vocabulary, verb + preposition combinations etc. which they can self-correct by checking their dictionaries. You could use a regular symbol e.g. >**D**, to indicate that students need to refer to their dictionary.

In general, encourage students to record as much of the information they get from their dictionary as possible in *Wordflo*. They could, for example, use the notes column in **A–Z** to record opposites, prepositions following verbs etc. They could also record example sentences from the dictionary in the **Vocabulary A–Z** 'Example Sentence' column or in **Grammar Dataflo**.

USEFUL PHRASES

Useful phrases is a personalised phrasebook and functions bank. Encourage students to look at the example pages, and to try to add some more phrases to them, before they create their own **Useful phrases** pages.

- **Aims**
- to encourage learners to create a phrasebook with expressions that are useful to them.
- to train learners to identify, record and use chunks of language that, with slight modifications, can be used again in particular speaking situations or written text-types.
- to train learners to record and distinguish between different registers (formal/informal, written/spoken, technical/non-technical, etc.).
- to allow learners to easily retrieve useful expressions when they need them in class, when studying alone, or when travelling.

- **Suggestion for use**

Time: 20 minutes.

1. When, in your textbook or course material, you are working on a dialogue (at a restaurant, on the phone, at the station, etc.), text-type (formal/informal letters, etc.), or function, draw a **Useful phrases** 'page' on the board.
2. The class suggests a maximum of six expressions from the text they think they might hear or say again in a similar situation. Write them on your 'page'.
3. Add any important information about pronunciation and/or register to the expressions on the board.
4. Students copy the 'page' on the board into **Useful phrases** in *Wordflo*.
5. The next time you work on a dialogue, text-type or function, encourage your students to add to **Useful phrases**.

- **Homework**

Students observe themselves in real-life situations (e.g. at the supermarket, at the gym, etc.), and note expressions they hear or use regularly. If they live in a country where English is not the main language, ask them to think about the phrases they use in everyday situations and how they would say those in English. Get open-class feedback in the next lesson.

GRAMMAR

GENERAL

There are various ways that the **Grammar** section can be used, for example:

1. As homework to support grammar work done in class.

2. By students at home, independently of what is being done in class, depending on what areas they feel they need to do more work on. In this case, it will be very helpful if they have the opportunity to give in their work to be checked from time to time i.e. the **Dataflo**, **About Me** and **Dataplus** sections. Where they make mistakes encourage them to add to their **Self-correction Data system**.

3. In class for revision (individual study). You may wish to encourage students to work on a different grammar area every week/ten days (or whatever is appropriate). Remind them that they should go back to earlier sections to add examples to the **Dataflo** and **Dataplus**.

From time to time, ask students about which of the **Grammar strategies** they are using/not using and why. Encourage them to try out particular strategies that they haven't used before.

USE and FORM

Ask students to read through these sections and to ask questions as necessary. Choose a grammar area that they have already covered in class. Remind students that if they want to get more information about any particular grammar point there are many suitable grammar reference materials e.g. Walker, E, Elsworth, S, *Grammar Practice for Intermediate Students*, Longman.

DATAFLO

Write on the board the key sentence from the **Dataflo** e.g. *We're visiting the Eiffel Tower tomorrow morning.* Ask students where the sentence might have originally come from (in this case, a postcard). Elicit the various sources of real English that students potentially have access to e.g. films, newspapers, radio, graded readers, the Internet etc. Tell them that the idea of **Dataflo** is that they become 'language researchers' and look out for and write down any examples of the relevant grammar structure in things they watch e.g. films, things they listen to e.g. songs, things they read e.g. newspapers, people they speak to e.g. their teacher.

If possible, bring extracts into class from newspapers, video etc. containing examples of relevant structures and get students to look/listen for them.

If you decide to use a particular part of the **Grammar** section with your whole class, you may like to set them the task of finding a certain number of examples for their **Dataflo** as homework. Then, in the next lesson, students can exchange examples they have found and the sources they have used.

Emphasise to students that they should regularly add to the different **Dataflo** sections as they come across new examples of target structures.

ABOUT ME

Complete the first one (truthfully if possible!) as an example to students of the kind of thing that is expected of them e.g. *This weekend I am visiting friends in (London)*. You may like to follow this up by getting all students to complete the first example in this section and then to 'mingle' with the other students in the class, comparing their sentences. They could then vote on who had the most interesting/unusual etc. sentence.

DATAPLUS

This section is for students to complete with additional examples of the target structure(s) of their own choosing/making. Ideally, students will construct sentences of most relevance to them and possibly which they will need to use in their everyday lives. It is likely that students will be able to remember the sentences better if they give them some kind of personal significance.

TESTING STUDENTS

When/if students complete all parts of the **Grammar section** you may like to:

1. Use the **Grammar check** as a test of how well students have understood the meaning of the various grammar areas.

2. Give students a 'Spot the Mistake' test where they identify a mistake of form in a series of sentences which incorporate the target structures you have been focusing on in class. See the example on the next page.

3. Test students on the **Irregular verbs list** at some point. It helps to reinforce meaning if you do it via gapped sentences (see test at the end of this section).

SPOT THE MISTAKE TEST

1. She doesn't drinks coffee in the mornings.
2. Is he haveing a shower?
3. They're going to playing football at the weekend.
4. When you will see Mike?
5. We were watching TV when Pete and Sarah were arriving.
6. I payed £50 for these shoes.
7. Have you ever drank champagne?
8. They've lived in Australia since a very long time.
9. If I go shopping, I buy some more orange juice.
10. If I had more time, I played tennis more often.
11. Could you give an information about train times, please?
12. He plays football very good.
13. That's the more expensive music system in the shop.
14. You musn't talk during this exam.
15. She can't to know we are here.

IRREGULAR VERBS TEST

1. Oh good, you've — your camera! (bring)
2. I'm really sorry. I — this glass last night. (break)
3. Have you — what you want to wear yet? (choose)
4. How much did that jacket — ? (cost)
5. She — from Cairo to Cape Town last summer. (drive)
6. I'm so hungry. I haven't — all day. (eat)
7. I — very sad when my best friend went abroad to study. (feel)
8. Oh, how embarrassing, I've — his name. (forget)
9. Have you — the news about Isabella? (hear)
10. Now, Carlos, why did you — your little brother? (hit)
11. I think you've — a serious mistake. (make)
12. I — your book on the kitchen table last night. (put)
13. He — in the last Olympics. (run)
14. I've had a fantastic time here in New York. Mel has — me all the sights. (show)
15. She — me a very nice letter on my birthday. (write)

SELF-CORRECTION

The **Self-correction Data system** helps students to learn from their errors. Learners record errors, corrected versions, or reformulations, of what they wanted to say or write. They can also add notes to explain their errors.

- **Aims**
  - to help learners gauge their progress by building a permanent record of the errors they make at different stages of their English learning.
  - to help learners build a permanent record of the explanations for errors and the correct versions of what they wanted to say or write, to help them avoid making the same mistakes.
  - to provide both the learner and the teacher with important feedback on which areas of the language the learner is having most problems with, and so needs more work on.

- **Selecting Errors to Record**

It is neither possible nor desirable for you to work on all your students' errors, so those recorded in this system should be carefully selected. Concentrate on:

  - errors from which unsuccessful communication might result.
  - typical, recurrent errors that many learners are making in class.
  - errors in a form just studied. If an exam is imminent, you will probably want learners to record and work on more errors than usual, including superficial ones, to help them avoid losing valuable marks.

- **Errors from written work**

Suggestion 1

1. Work out errors on the board, as a whole-class activity.
2. Students then write them in their **Self-correction Data systems**.

Suggestion 2

1. Make a note of frequent errors. Enter these into a **Self-correction** page. In the Notes column give an explanation of the error. Do not give the correction.

2. Photocopy and distribute.

3. In pairs or groups, students complete the corrected versions. With stronger groups, don't provide the explanation of the error. Let them work it out for themselves and then record it in the appropriate column in **Self-correction**.

Suggestion 3
1. Students write down five errors they made in a recent piece of written work. Alternatively, indicate in your corrections exactly which errors they should record.
2. Students analyse, discuss, and work on the errors in pairs or in groups and write in the correct versions and any notes that will help them.

VOCABULARY GAMES

DEFINITION GAME
Time: 5–15 minutes

1. Ask one student to sit facing away from you.
2. Hold up a card with a word or phrase on it that students have recently learnt. The rest of the class can see what is written on the card.
3. The class calls out definitions and synonyms to help the individual student guess what is written on the card.

MAKING MATCHES
Time: 15–30 minutes

1. Make a set of cards, a minimum of twelve, from the vocabulary and expressions that students have recorded. Use words with prefixes, phrasal verbs, power verbs, and word partners. Write one part of each word or expression on different cards so that students have to match up the two halves.

Example	im	possible
	put	off
	get	over
	have	time
	cold	weather

2. Divide students into pairs. Give each pair a set of cards.
3. Students have to match the cards to make correct combinations.

Variation
1. Use new word combinations on the cards.
2. Students use their dictionaries to find out which halves match.
3. Get feedback.
4. Students record the new words and expressions in their *Wordflo*.

ANAGRAMS

Time: 5–15 minutes

1. Divide the class into pairs or teams. Give students anagrams of single words or expressions. You can write these on the board or on cards or give out a photocopied list.
   Example   veha a yptar
                  od lewl
   (Answers: have a party, do well)

2. Students decode the anagrams. The first pair or team to do so are the winners.

Variation
Students make anagrams for each other.

WORDPLAY WARMERS

Time: 10–15 minutes

1. At the beginning of the lesson, students look through the vocabulary section of their *Wordflo,* and pick out words that they like. On the board, write the following options:
   - *Think of a word that rhymes with it.*
   - *Find a word that means the same.*
   - *Find a word that means the opposite.*
   - *Use it correctly in a sentence.*
   - *Ask an interesting question with it.*
   - *Spell it in less than 10 seconds.*
   - *Spell it backwards in less than 20 seconds.*
   - *Make as many words as you can from the word (verbs, nouns, adjectives, etc. prefixes and suffixes are allowed).*

2. The first student reads his/her word twice. Invite students to accept the challenge on the board. The first student who raises his/her hand attempts to do all the tasks on the board, receiving 1 point for each correct answer (1/2 point for each word in option 8). Each student has only one turn in each session (so that the same students do not always volunteer).

3. Give students time to add to and change the information in their **Data systems**.

4. (Optional) You can open several classes with this game, and keep a running score. This will encourage students to study their records more.

Variation
Open the challenge up to the whole class, rather than one student at a time, so that one student might volunteer a rhyme, another a synonym, and so on. Score accordingly.

WORD HANGMAN

Time: 15–20 minutes

1. Divide the class into two teams.
2. Each team chooses a word from one of their *Wordflos*.
3. The teams take it in turns to send a member up to the board. The student at the board draws a line for each letter of the word.
4. The opposing team calls out letters. If the letters are included in the word, the student fills these in. If they are not she/he constructs the following diagram, one line for each 'incorrect' letter. The team aims to complete the word before they are hanged. Students have to remember which incorrect letters have already been suggested so that they do not repeat these.

   Once they have a number of letters filled in, they can guess what the word is. If they are wrong, the student marks in another line to hang them.

   p _ _ t _ _ _ _ _ p h e r

   Answer: photographer

5. Students record any new words that interest them in (an) appropriate **Data system(s)** in *Wordflo*.

SENTENCE HANGMAN

Time: 15 – 20 minutes

1. As above, but the teams choose sentences, rather than single words, from their *Wordflos*. The student at the board draws a line for each word of the sentence, and the opposing team calls out words until they complete the sentence or get "hanged".

2. Students record any new words, expressions or sentences that interest them in (an) appropriate **Data system(s)** in their *Wordflo*.

TOPIC QUICKFIRE

Time: 10 –15 minutes

1. Give students a topic e.g. animals.
2. Students sit in a circle.
3. Each student thinks of an animal, but doesn't say what it is at this point.
4. Students clap in rhythm like this: both hands on knees, clap hands, click fingers on left hand, click fingers on right hand. Ensure that this rhythm is established before the game starts.
5. Start by saying the name of an animal, or whatever the topic is, after you have clicked fingers on your right hand.
6. Students have to say the name of an animal after clicking their fingers on left hand. The name they give must not duplicate any of the names already given. If students miss a 'click', or can't think of a word or duplicate a word, then they fall out of the game.
7. Students record any words which are new to them.

Follow-up
Play the game as above, but students have to say one of the words they heard from another student in the first round.

WORD ASSOCIATION

Time: 10–15 minutes

Follow the same procedure as for **Topic quickfire**, but instead of choosing a topic allow students to make associations between words.

Example   Teacher: Snow
                Student 1: White.
                Student 2: Teeth.
                Student 3: Dentist.
                Student 4: Pain.
                Student 5: Hospital.
                Student 6: Building.

DON'T SAY IT!

Time: 15–30 minutes

1. Students choose six words from their *Wordflo*. For each word they write this word and four related words on a card.

   Example   SPORT
   - play
   - game
   - match
   - football

2. Divide the class into two teams, A and B.

3. Team A gives their cards to Team B, and vice versa.

4. One team-member then has to explain to his/her team the main word on his/her card (e.g. SPORT) without using that word, or any of the four related words. If the team can guess the word within two minutes, they get 2 points. If they can't, or if the person explaining uses one of the four words on the card, they lose 2 points.

5. Continue with other cards, alternating Team A – Team B.

6. Students record new words that interest them in (an) appropriate **Data system(s)** in their *Wordflo*.

7. (Optional) Students make new cards for a future game.

VOCABULARY BINGO

Time: 15–20 minutes

1. Students look through their *Wordflo* and call out items they have recently learnt that they would like to review.

2. Write their suggestions on the board, until you have about twenty-five items.

3. Each student chooses five of these words/expressions and writes them down.

4. Call out definitions of the words/expressions on the board at random. When students think they hear one of their chosen items, they cross it out.

5. The first student to cross out all of their items shouts "Bingo!". Ask the student to read out the words/expressions so that you can check.

6. Ask the winner to define five words/expressions.

7. (Optional) Repeat the game or continue the game to find a second- and third-place winner.

Acknowledgement: Adapted from *Games for Language Learning*, CUP by Wright, Betteridge and Buckby.

NAME TWO THINGS

Time: 20–30 minutes

1. Give out a handout similar to the example opposite, based on vocabulary students have covered.

2. Give students 15–20 minutes to fill in as much as they can. Keep posting the time on the board to keep the pace fast and the students working quickly.

3. Get feedback from students. Resolve spelling and pronunciation problems.

4. Students write the new vocabulary that they learn from other students in appropriate **Data systems** in *Wordflo*.

NAME TWO THINGS

Name at least two things that:

1. open and close.
2. taste bitter.
3. are red.
4. are round.
5. always come in pairs.
6. are usually made of wood.
7. you can find on an office desk.
8. you can wear on your hands.
9. make loud, unpleasant noises.
10. are always cold.
11. are small enough to fit in your pocket.
12. you can use for cutting.
13. are dangerous.
14. children usually do.
15. many people are afraid of.

Photocopiable

WORD SEARCH

Time: 20–30 minutes

1. Divide the class into two teams, A and B, and the teams into pairs.
2. Give each pair an empty grid (10 squares x 10 squares if you use grid paper), with a list of words at the bottom related to a topic you want to focus on.
3. Set the rules for the **Word search** (hidden words can run up, down, diagonally or back-to-front).
4. Get the pairs to compose Word searches on their grids (maximum ten to fifteen words).
   Example

U	X	T	R	J	H	K	C	S	U
Q	P	G	F	E	D	U	O	L	Z
R	O	U	V	X	W	D	P	F	E
I	P	I	T	V	D	Z	H	I	J
D	A	T	C	P	N	R	M	L	F
Q	O	A	L	C	R	G	U	V	S
Q	P	R	L	D	N	X	F	M	J
J	Q	M	F	V	R	N	L	D	S
I	N	S	T	R	U	M	E	N	T
F	Q	V	F	E	R	P	L	M	N

5. When they are ready, the pairs exchange their grids with pairs from the opposing team.
6. The pairs try to solve the **Word search** that their opponents have set them.
7. Students record any new vocabulary in the **Topic pages** and/or **Word webs**.

DEFINITION GAME

Time: 15–30 minutes

1. Prepare a set of cards with vocabulary that students have recently learnt. Copy these so you have enough sets for each team.
2. Divide the class into teams with four students in each team and give each team a set of cards. Each team sits in a circle.
3. One student in each team picks up a card, but does not show it to the rest of the team. The student defines or gives a synonym of the word so that the rest of the team guess the word. She/he can give some context e.g.: *Everyone was crying because the film was very ....*
   (Answer: sad)
   Monitor to ensure that the definitions students give are correct.
4. If the other students guess the word, the first student puts the card down and the next student picks up the next card. The procedure is repeated.
   If, however, the student cannot define the word or expression or the other team members cannot guess it, then the student puts the card back at the bottom of the pack and picks up a second card. If this second attempt is also unsuccessful, the second student picks up a card.
5. The first team to define all their cards successfully is the winner.

TRUE OR FALSE?

Time: 20 minutes

Stage 1
1. Write on cards a word or expression that students have recently encountered.
2. Divide the class into groups of three or four students.
3. Give each group a card.

4. Give students three definitions for the word or expression.
5. Students discuss in groups which is the correct meaning.
6. Feedback and ask students to use the word in a sentence.
7. Record new expressions in *Wordflo*.

Stage 2
Time: 15–30 minutes

1. Divide the class into two teams.
2. Students choose words from *Wordflo* and write three definitions for each word. Two definitions should be false and one should be true.

   They could refer in particular to **A–Z**, **Phrasal verbs** and **Power verbs** where they will have already written in meanings.

   For the false meanings, students can refer to monolingual dictionaries or write out the meanings of other words/expressions they have recorded in *Wordflo*.
3. The students then read out their words and definitions to the other team who have to guess the correct answer.
   Score points when they guess correctly.

VOCABULARY BATTLE
Time: 30 minutes

1. Divide the class into two or four groups and give them a set time to produce a list of vocabulary for a specific topic e.g. jobs, items of clothing.
2. Students work together to produce a list of as many words as possible. Monitor and check there are no mistakes, that they know what the word means and that it is relevant to the topic. Each student will need to make a copy of the list.
3. Pair each student with someone from a different group. Students must not show their lists to each other yet.

4. Students read through their lists and score a point for each word which they've got that is not on the other student's list. Students must be able to correctly pronounce, define and 'teach' this word to score the point.

Variation

If this activity is repeated with the same group, students may start to choose very obscure and therefore less useful vocabulary in order to score a point. To avoid this, ask the two groups to make lists on different topics. When each group has finished ask each group to guess what is on the other group's list. Students could produce a **Word web** rather than a list.

PICTURE REVIEW

Time: 30–45 minutes

1. Cut out at least thirty magazine pictures, especially unusual or strange ones. Mount them on cardboard so that you can use them again.

2. Write out the vocabulary items you want to review on separate cards. Use vocabulary which you have covered and that students have recorded in *Wordflo*.

3. In class, spread all the pictures out on a desk or table. If you do not have a big enough desk, spread all the pictures on the floor.

4. Give each student two to three cards. (Give stronger students more to keep them busy). Keep one or two for yourself to demonstrate the activity.

5. Students check the meanings of items they don't remember in their *Wordflo* or with each other. (Make sure they can correctly ask "What does _____ mean?")

6. Students then place their cards on the different pictures, according to associations they can make between the vocabulary items and the pictures. (Give an example with the cards you kept in step 4.)

7. When everyone has finished, all the students look at the

vocabulary/picture combinations and ask about any associations that are not immediately clear. The students who placed those cards explain their reasons.

QUIZ SHOW

Time: 30 – 40 minutes

1. Prepare four different vocabulary lists – lists A, B, C, and D – with five to eight words on each which students have recently learned.

2. Divide the class into groups of four. Seat them in the following manner, with A and B facing, and C and D facing.

3. Give A and B their vocabulary lists, face down.

4. When you say "go", both students turn over their lists and have ten minutes to get each other to guess the items on their lists. They can use synonyms, definitions, examples, or mime, but they may not spell. Stress that they are not competing against each other, but against the other pair, and that they have ten minutes for both of the lists. They should not waste time on items they can't remember or can't get the other student to guess.

5. C and D keep track of the score: 1 point for each word which is guessed correctly.

6. After ten minutes, give C and D their lists and repeat steps 3 and 4. This time, A and B listen and keep the score.

7. After the game, go through all of the lists. Students explain to the class how they successfully communicated the words.

MIND STORY

Time: steps 1 – 4, 30 minutes; step 5, 15 minutes

1. Put a maximum of twenty new words/expressions (for example, items that students will need for a later reading/listening/discussion activity) in a box or circle on the board or on a photocopied hand-out.

2. Elicit/teach the meanings of the new items.

3. Give students five minutes to create a story in their minds, using all the words in any order.

4. When the five minutes are up, students tell each other their stories in pairs or small groups.

5. Some of the pairs/groups tell their stories to the whole class.

6. Students record the new words in *Wordflo*.

7. (Optional) Students write up the story, in class or for homework.

Variation

1. Instead of telling each other their stories, students write them on loose-leaf paper (coloured if possible).

2. When they have finished writing, they put their stories up on the wall around the room and circulate, reading each others' work.

3. Students report back to the class on why they liked particular stories they read.

GRAMMAR GAMES

GRAMMAR AUCTION

1. Elicit from students what an 'auction' is and what happens at an auction i.e. that various things are put up for sale and the highest bidder gets them. However, sometimes there are 'fake' items and obviously you don't want to buy those.

2. Put students in pairs and explain that you are going to have a '<u>Grammar</u> Auction'. Each pair of students will have £2000 to bid with and they will be bidding for grammatically correct sentences.

3. Give students a handout with twelve to fifteen sentences containing structures they have recently been studying in class. Some of the sentences should be correct and some should have a grammatical mistake.

4. You (the teacher) become the 'auctioneer' and auction off the sentences one by one. The students, in their pairs, bid (or don't bid!) for each sentence. They should bid in amounts of £100. The winning pair of students are those with the most correct sentences and the most money by the end of the 'auction'.

Acknowledgement: *Grammar Games,* CUP by Mario Rinvolucri.

GRAMMAR CLOZE

1. Prepare a short text e.g. 50–90 words which incorporates a number of examples of the grammatical structures that you have recently been focusing on in class. (You might decide to adapt a text that you have used from your coursebook.)

2. Give students an idea of the general content of the text either via the title or a supporting picture or a very brief oral summary.

3. Put up a gapped version of the text on the board or on OHP. One space for each missing word.

4. Divide students into teams (or do this a whole class activity).

5. Nominate a spokesperson for each team.

6. The teams in turn suggest one missing word. If the word they

suggest appears in the text, write it in each place that it appears and give the teams the number of points for the number of times that the word appears. So, if they say 'the' and 'the' appears in the text five times, they score 5 points. Continue until the text is complete.

Example:

Letter to a pen-pal about everyday routine

Dear Maria,

.... letter.
.... everyday routine ....
....

I get up at .... in the week. I want to swim .... Britain .... Olympics and I .... to train every day! .... breakfast I always have tea and some toast and .... School starts at 9.00.a.m. and finishes at .... I .... more swimming .... school but I usually .... home .... 6.00.p.m. .... always have dinner at 7.00.p.m. and then I do .... homework. I don't .... to watch TV ....

Complete version

> **Letter to a pen-pal about everyday routine**
>
> Dear Maria,
> Thank you for your letter. Your everyday routine is very different to mine.
>
> I get up at 5.00 a.m. in the week. I want to swim for Britain in the next Olympics and I have to train every day! For breakfast I always have tea and some toast and marmalade. School starts at 9.00 a.m. and finishes at 4.00 p.m. I do more swimming after school but I usually get home by 6.00 p.m. We always have dinner at 7.00 p.m. and then I do my homework. I don't often have time to watch TV unfortunately.

GRAMMAR NOUGHTS AND CROSSES

1. Draw a 'noughts and crosses' board on the board.

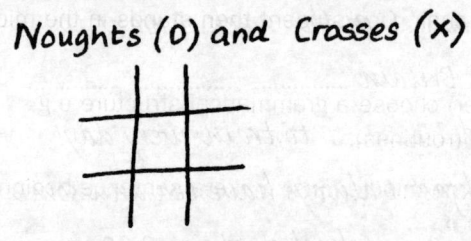

   Noughts (O) and Crosses (X)

2. Divide students into two teams.
3. Nominate a spokesperson for each team and then get them to play a game of 'noughts and crosses' against each other. You place each team's nought or cross where you are instructed.
   The aim of the game is for each team to try and get a line of three noughts or three crosses in a row – horizontally, vertically or diagonally.

4. Explain that you are going to play a slightly different version of the same game, called 'grammar noughts and crosses'. In this version, students must answer a grammar question before they are allowed to place their nought or cross. So, for example, Team A (noughts) begins and gets the question: What is the past participle of the verb *steal*?

5. If they answer correctly (*stolen*), then they can choose where to place their nought e.g. in the top right hand corner. If they can't answer the question correctly then it becomes Team B's (crosses) turn and they receive a new question.

6. The game continues until again, one team manages to get a line of three noughts or three crosses in a row – horizontally, vertically or diagonally.

GRAMMAR MUSICAL CHAIRS

1. Put out chairs for everyone in the class in a circle.

2. Take away one chair. One student then stands in the middle of the circle.

3. You (the teacher) choose a grammatical structure e.g. Present simple (routines).

4. The student in the middle must make a sentence beginning: **Change places if ....**
   Example: *Change places if you have coffee for breakfast*.

5. Those students who do have coffee for breakfast must stand up and move to another seat. The student in the middle should also find a seat to sit in. The student who fails to find a seat then stands in the middle and constructs a new sentence using the target structure. The teacher can decide to change the target structure from time to time.

   Examples of possible structures:
   Present simple (routines) e.g.
   Change places if you watch TV every night.
   Past simple e.g.
   Change places if you went to a disco last night.
   'Going to' (future plans) e.g.

Change places if you are going to play a sport this weekend.
Present perfect (experience) e.g.
Change places if you have ever been to America.
Adverbs (manner) e.g.
Change places if you can sing well.
Should e.g.
Change places if you think smoking should be banned in public places.

TELL IT AGAIN

1. Prepare or find a short text (100–150 words) at the students' level and containing several examples of the structure/structures you want to concentrate on. Anecdotes work well because there is a clear storyline to follow.
2. Elicit/pre-teach new vocabulary items and write them on the board.
3. Read the text once. Students do not take notes at this time; they just attempt to follow and understand.
4. Read the text again. Students take notes. Emphasise that this is not a dictation, and that students should only write keywords.
5. Read the text one more time while students again take notes.
6. Put students in groups of three or four. They choose a secretary to write.
7. Students must reconstruct the text. The text does not have to be exactly the same (in fact, this is probably impossible), but all the information must be there.
8. Monitor and help.
9. Collect the papers and correct them for the next lesson.
10. In the next lesson, give back the corrected papers to the groups. Discuss the problems they had with the target structure(s). Then give out the original text. Discuss the differences between their versions and the original text.